COPYRIGHT INFORMATION BULLETIN SERIES:

1. Jerome K. Miller, *Using Copyrighted Videocassettes in Classrooms and Libraries*, 1984 (out of print).

2. Charles W. Vlcek, *Copyright Policy Development: A Resource Book for Educators*, 1987.

3. Jerome K. Miller, *Using Copyrighted Videocassettes in Classrooms, Libraries, and Training Centers*, (scheduled for late 1987).

4. Esther R. Sinofsky, *Copyright Handbook for Film, Video, and Multi-image Production*, (scheduled for 1987).

COPYRIGHT POLICY DEVELOPMENT:
A RESOURCE BOOK FOR EDUCATORS

by

Dr. Charles W. Vlcek

COPYRIGHT INFORMATION SERVICES

PJC LEARNING RESOURCES CENTER

Published and distributed by:

COPYRIGHT INFORMATION SERVICES
P.O. Box 1460
Friday Harbor, WA 98250
Phone: (206) 378-5128

ISBN: 0-91413-08-5

Series: Copyright Information Bulletin, No.2

DISCLAIMER: The opinions contained herein reflect the author's informed opinion but do not constitute legal advice.

88 - 2013

Dedicated to my wife Evelyn for her encouragement, and to my children Jeannette, Tim and Beverly for their patience in sharing my time.

COPYRIGHT POLICY DEVELOPMENT: A RESOURCE BOOK FOR EDUCATORS

INTRODUCTION

The Copyright Law, Public Law 94-553, passed in 1976 and was implemented on January 1, 1978. While the law is wrought with ambiguities in its rhetoric and application to education, educators will surely agree that a revision of the 1909 law was necessary. The 1909 law did not reflect the instructional materials and technology available in the 1970's. In fact, the existing technology could not even have been imagined then.

The 1976 Copyright Revision Act is very confusing and seems to be written to provide a "guaranteed income for copyright lawyers." Recent court cases seem to create more confusion about these issues. Most copyright infringements are settled out of court to save time, money, and publicity. Although this is a practical practice, it impedes legal clarification of the issues by the courts.

Some help can be found in the three fair-use guidelines for educators developed by representatives of the creating, producing, labor, and educational communities. While the guidelines provide **minimal** criteria, they do not provide complete guidance to educators regarding duplication of instructional materials for classroom use. The texts of the three guidelines are reprinted in several sources, including: *The Official Fair-Use Guidelines: Complete Texts...* available from Copyright Information Services, P.O. Box 1460, Friday Harbor, WA 98250.

Administrators of many schools and colleges are now impressing upon their teachers the importance of observing the copyright law. Most institutions do this by issuing copyright policies for their staff to follow. By implementing copyright policies, the administrators hope to avoid potential litigation problems for their staff, institution, and themselves.

To obtain a better understanding of the development of educational copyright policies, I wrote to the senior educational media professional in each State Department of Education, asking for the names of schools, colleges and universities in their state that might have outstanding copyright policies. I also wrote to the President and Immediate Past President of each state library media association requesting the same information. Respondents were asked to nominate institutions with excellent copyright policies at the (1) school district, (2) intermediate or educational service district, and (3) college and university levels. They also were asked to identify policies governing the use of television satellite systems. Forty-five school districts, intermediate or educational service districts, colleges and universities were nominated, with almost all of them at the school district or college and university levels. No exemplary television satellite policies were identified. Letters were then sent to each nominee requesting a copy of their copyright policy. Twenty-eight institutions submitted policies. These were carefully reviewed and a limited number were selected for inclusion in this book. Based upon their contents and the author's experience, copyright policy guidelines were developed.

The purpose of this book is to provide guidelines for colleges, universities and schools to use when writing a copyright policy. The following information will be provided:

1. Guidelines for writing a copyright policy.
2. Guidelines for implementing the policy.
3. Current information pertaining to the educational use of programs by satellite reception.
4. Selected examples of existing copyright policies.
5. Selected bibliography of current articles related to copyright policy development.

ACKNOWLEDGMENTS

Many people contributed to the preparation of this book. Dr. William D. Schmidt suggested the methodology for identifying and obtaining the exemplary copyright policies. One hundred thirty-two library media administrators were contacted with twenty-four correspondents nominating forty-five institutions who were perceived as having excellent copyright policies. The book would not have been complete without the help of the people who shared their institutional copyright policies with me, especially those whose institution's policies are included in this book: Ann Barrett, Lane Community College, Eugene, Oregon; Boyd Geer, Madison Public Schools, Madison, Wisconsin; Donald Hess, Granite School District, Salt Lake City, Utah; Glenn C. Kessler, Prince William County Public Schools, Manassas, Virginia; Ray Stansbury, Grossmont Union High School District, La Mesa, California; and my own institution, Central Washington University, Ellensburg, Washington. Finally, Jerome K. Miller encouraged me to write this book and carefully reviewed its contents. My thanks to all of them.

The author sincerely hopes the readers will find the ideas, information, and copyright policies presented in this book helpful.

Charles Vlcek

CHAPTER I:

THE NEED FOR A COPYRIGHT POLICY

The past decade brought educators new tools to make quick, quality copies of all types of teaching materials. The practice of copying these materials for classroom use is deeply instilled and accepted by classroom teachers. Educators want to bring excellent and appropriate materials to their classrooms and to their students at the "teachable moment." Given the tight budgets prevalent in educational institutions, it is no wonder that educators are tempted to infringe the copyright law by excessive copying.

On the other hand, we cannot blame the creators of these materials for crying foul, and insisting on an adequate financial return on their investments. After investing time and money in producing these materials, they should expect a reasonable return on their investments. That's the American Way! Without the creating industries, instructional materials would disappear. Their interests must be protected for the ultimate good of education!

To protect their interests, publishers and media producers have begun putting pressure on educational institutions to correct abuses of copyrighted materials. While a few cases are brought to trial, and consequently to the attention of the press, many cases are threatened and settled out of court through a "consent decree" which minimizes expenses and unfavorable publicity. Although this is a practical approach for both parties, it fails to develop case law affecting educators. Only one case was resolved recently by the courts. In that case, the Erie County New York Board of Cooperative Educational Services (BOCES) was found guilty of copyright infringments in videotaping, duplicating, and distributing television programs videotaped from a local Public Television station. The case cost the BOCES $78,000, plus court costs and legal fees. Each board member and employee associated with the infringing activities was named in the suit. The court costs and legal fees paid by the BOCES is reliably reported to have exceeded the $78,000 in damages levied by the court.

There may be still other longterm costs to institutions as a condition of out-of-court settlements (consent decrees) which may be more costly than the monetary value of the settlement. The institution may have to agree to surrender or greatly curtail their fair-use rights. As a part of the settlement, the institution is likely to have to agree to stop videotaping off the air or curtail their fair-use right to make photocopies. Over a period of years, these limitations represent a substantial educational and monetary loss.

The Training Media Producers Association, a trade association of media producers, is attempting to curtail copyright violations by offering rewards for information leading to the prosecution of copyright infringers. Rewards are quite an incentive for disgruntled students, parents, or staff members who find the reward attractive or who want to "get even" with an institution or colleagues.

The Federal Bureau of Investigation investigates alleged copyright infringements. The author is aware of two cases in the Pacific Northwest where FBI agents entered schools to investigate alleged copyright infringements. In both instances the charges were settled out of court. In one instance, the media director lost her job as a result of the out-of-court settlement.

The threat of a lawsuit is not the only reason institutions

2

should discourage copyright violations. There is also the ethical issue of "setting an example." Teachers are expected to be role models for their students. Therefore, violating the copyright law may be considered as stealing as it may deprive creators of their royalties. When teachers and administrators violate the copyright law, students get the impression that breaking the law is okay, as long as no one gets caught.

There are many remedies for copyright infringement: (1) injunctions, (2) impounding and disposition of infringing articles, (3) damages and profits, (4) court costs and attorney's fees, and (5) criminal offenses. An infringer of the copyright law may be found liable for (1) the copyright owner's actual damages and any other additional profits of the infringer (Title 17, *United States Code*, Sect. 504(a)(2)), or (2) statutory damages where civil damages of not less than $250 or more than $10,000 per infringement (Sect. 504(c)(1)). For willful violations **for financial gain**, criminal penalties can be assessed including imprisonment and larger monetary fines. An "innocent infringer" provision is provided for educators who can demonstrate they were not aware and had no reason to believe the action was an infringement (Sect. 504(c)(2)). However, the innocent infringer may be held responsible for the court costs and attorney fees, which can be substantial.

When a complaint is brought against an institution, the document names (1) the alleged infringer (the person doing the infringing), (2) the legal entity responsible for the institution (the governing board), (3) the chief executive, and (4) contributory infringers (teachers, department heads, deans, principals, media specialists, etc.). "A contributory infringer is one who, with knowledge of the infringing activity, induces, causes or materially contributed to the infringing conduct of another." (*Gershwin Pub. Corp.* v. *Columbia Artists Management, Inc.*, 443 F.2d 1158, 1162 (1921) quoted in: *Encyclopedia Britannica Educational Corp., et al.* v. *C.N. Crooks, et al.*, Order of March 10, 1983, p. 20). "A defendant's mistakes as to the legal consequences of his actions do not constitute an excuse for an infringement. It is only necessary that a copyright defendant have knowledge of the infringing activity." (*Universal City*

Studios v. *Sony Corp. of America,* 659 F.2d at 975, quoted in: *Encyclopedia Britannica Educational Corp., et al.* v. *C.N. Crooks, et al.,* Order of March 10, 1983, pp. 20-21). Contributory infringers include colleagues who assist in an infringement or administrators who know of an infringement and fail to take appropriate steps to stop it.

Because of the current trend toward copyright litigation, and to protect themselves against copyright litigation, administrators in many educational institutions are developing copyright policies to affix responsibility within the school's hierarchy. A copyright policy not only protects the administration but informs employees of what they can and cannot do regarding duplication and use of copyrighted materials.

CHAPTER II:

COPYRIGHT POLICY DEVELOPMENT

Once the decision has been made to develop an institutional copyright policy one asks, what should the copyright policy contain? After reviewing twenty-eight policies submitted to the author, several elements became apparent in the better policies. The statements varied widely; some were extremely brief while others were extremely lengthy. However, the best seemed to include (1) a short, concise **policy statement** and (2) a lengthy **copyright manual**. The best copyright manuals were comprehensive, and they must be if they are to be meaningful for employees. The review identified the following major elements that should be included in an institution's copyright policy.

1. A statement that the board intends to abide by the Copyright Law (Title 17, *United States Code*, Sect. 101, et seq.).

This statement does not need to be long. It needs only to recognize that the copyright law exists and simply state that the institution and its employees are obliged legally to abide by the law.

Example: It is the intent of the Board/Trustees to adhere to the provisions of the U.S. Copyright Law (Title 17, *United States Code*, Sect. 101, et seq.). Though there continues to be controversy regarding interpretation of the copyright law, this policy represents a sincere effort to operate legally. The Board/Trustees directs the administration to provide district employees with guidelines that clearly discourage violation of copyright law.

2. A statement prohibiting copying not specifically allowed by the copyright law, fair use guidelines, license agreement, or the permission of the copyright proprietor.

None of the policy statements received in this survey addressed all of these elements. Most policies mentioned Fair Use (Sect. 107), the three fair use guidelines, and written permission. Policy developers should remember that the law also provides legal copying through Section 108 (Reproductions by Libraries and Archives); Section 110 (Exemption of Certain Performances and Displays); and Section 117 (Computer Programs). License agreements also must be considered as licensing is now commonly used to permit local duplication and use of copyrighted materials.

Example: The Board/Trustees prohibit the institution's employees from copying materials not specifically allowed by the (1) copyright law, (2) fair use guidelines, (3) licenses or contractural agreements, or (4) other permission. All other copying must have the written permission of the institution's copyright officer.

3. A statement that places the liability for willful infringement upon the person requesting the work.

Without such a statement, any copyright policy will be weak. If employees are not held personally responsible for their actions, they will not adhere to the policy. On the other hand, the term "willful" should be included so if the individual can prove that he/she had defensible reasons to believe that the copying met the institution's policy, then the institution should be willing to support the individual. Without the inclusion of the term, employees may decide not to take the risk and avoid all copying, even though it may be legal.

Example: The Board/Trustees disapproves of unauthorized duplication in any form. Employees who willfully disregard

6

the copyright policy are in violation of Board/Trustee Policy, and do so at their own risk and assume all liability.

4. A statement that names a Copyright Officer for the Institution.

The copyright officer should be responsible for the administration of the institution's copyright policy. He/she should be someone in a position with authority, i.e., assistant superintendent, vice president, dean of instruction, curriculum director, or one who is clearly given the authority throughout the organization. The person must be in a position to speak with authority for the administration. The copyright officer must be readily available to answer copyright inquiries, advise employees about copyright matters, and hold copyright workshops to inform employees of their responsibilities. The employer may not be able to hold employees responsible for their actions if the institution does not educate the employees and respond to their questions. The copyright officer must assure that appropriate and adequate copyright procedures and records are created, implemented and maintained. The copyright officer should also serve as liaison with the institution's legal counsel on all copyright matters. Large school districts and multi-campus universities may wish to appoint deputy copyright officers for each campus.

Example: The Dean of Instruction/Assistant Superintendent is hereby named as the Copyright Officer with the responsibility to establish and implement appropriate procedures, prepare and distribute a copyright manual, and conduct training programs to assure that district personnel are advised on the current copyright law so that they can perform their duties within the intent of the law.

5. A statement that mandates the development of a copyright manual detailing what copying can and cannot be done by the institution's employees.

A copyright manual is needed and should be created for employee use. Without a manual, it is difficult to hold employees responsible for their actions. The manual must fully describe what copying can and cannot be done. It should include reference to appropriate sections of the copyright law and current fair use guidelines. While most of the policy examples submitted to the author included copyright information necessary for employees, none placed this information in a separate employee copyright manual. The author believes it would be better to separate the manual from the policy as policies tend to be stable and change infrequently, while the manual must be revised to remain current as the law is amended, as new technology appears, and as the courts clarify the law.

Example: The copyright officer shall develop and keep current a copyright manual designed to inform employees of their rights and responsibilities under the copyright law.

6. Appropriate notices shall be placed on or near all equipment capable of making copies of copyrighted material.

A warning notice should be placed on or near all equipment which can be used to make copies of copyrighted works that will be visible to anyone using the device. Copying devices include photocopiers, mimeograph and ditto machines, transparency makers, audio recorders, video recorders, photographic copy stands, microfilm reader/printers, and computers. Different notices are required in places where employees accept orders for copies and where self-service copiers are available.

A library that makes copies FOR patrons must prominently display the warning notice in Appendix III-A at the place where orders are taken. The copyright warning notices should be printed on plastic or heavy paper and in type of at least 18 points in size. This notice also must be placed on order forms in a box adjacent to the space calling for the name or signature of the person requesting the copy. The print size on the notice shall be no smaller than that used on the rest of the form and in no smaller than 8 point (Sect. 108(d)(2)).

Libraries also are required to place a notice of copyright on the first page of any copy they make for a patron (Sect. 108(a)(2)). The law does not prescribe the language but the American Library Association (ALA) suggests the warning

8

notice shown in Appendix III-B.

A copyright warning notice also must be posted near UNSUPERVISED copying equipment in libraries to advise persons that the duplication of a copyrighted work may be a copyright infringement (Sect. 108(f)(1)). While the language again is not specified in the law, the warning notice recommended by the ALA appears in Appendix III-C. The copying equipment in question includes, but is not limited to, photographic, reprographic or paper copy machines, audio duplicators, microform copiers, or video duplicators. These machines may be coin operated or actuated in any other manner. It is suggested further that borrowers of equipment that may be used for copying also be advised that such use of the equipment may be a violation of the copyright law. Many institutions use adhesive labels that can be attached to machines for this purpose.

Example: The Board/Trustees mandate that appropriate copyright notices by placed on or near all equipment capable of duplicating copyrighted materials.

7. A statement that mandates that adequate copyright records be maintained regarding permissions, responses to requests and license agreements.

The copyright officer should be responsible for maintaining suitable records of licenses, permissions, off air duplication, etc. While individual teachers and faculty members may be given the responsibility to obtain simple permissions, retention of copies of those permissions and the development of license agreements must be the responsibility of one officer. License agreements can be very complex and involve much negotiating. An institution should not permit each staff member to negotiate for a multitude of different and potentially duplicate agreements. This procedure could result in mass confusion. If copyright records are not centralized in one office it may be very difficult to retrieve necessary records and agreements when needed.

Example: The Board/Trustees mandate that the copyright officer maintain appropriate records regarding the use of copyrighted materials by employees.

SUMMARY

A review of the better copyright policies submitted to the author indicated that an institution's copyright policy should contain the following elements:

1. A statement that the board intends to abide by the Copyright Law.

2. A statement prohibiting copying not specifically allowed by the copyright law, fair use guidelines, license agreements, or proprietor's permission.

3. A statement placing the liability for willful infringement upon the person making or requesting the copy.

4. A statement that creates the position of copyright officer for the institution.

5. A statement mandating the development of a copyright manual detailing what copying can and cannot be done by the institution's employees.

6. A statement mandating placement of appropriate notices on or near all equipment capable of making copies.

7. A statement mandating the development and retention of appropriate copyright records.

CHAPTER III:

IMPLEMENTING THE POLICY

Once the School Board or Trustees adopt a Copyright Policy, it must be properly implemented. Responsibility for compliance must be assigned and employees must be informed. The following steps are suggested as an effective method to implement copyright policy.

1. Develop the Copyright Policy.

The first step in implementing a copyright policy is to develop the policy. By studying and following the suggestions and copyright policy examples presented in this book one should be able to develop an effective copyright policy the Board/Trustees can adopt. The policy should comply with the copyright law (Title 17, *United States Code*, Sect. 101 et seq.) and the finished document should be reviewed by the institution's legal counsel. Please note that the author did not suggest that legal counsel **write** the policy. A better policy, and one that reflects the needs of teachers, should result if it is written by educators who know the problems of teaching and how instructional materials are used in teaching. Lawyers are not trained as educators and educators are not trained as lawyers. Legal counsel and educators must work together as a team to develop and write an effective policy.

11

2. Develop a Copyright Manual For the Institution's Employees.

The Copyright Manual implements the trustees' or board's copyright policy. This manual should be very specific and inform employees what they can and cannot do regarding the use and copying of copyrighted materials. It should be organized for easy use by a variety of employees. Suggested chapters are: (1) The Purpose of the Copyright Law, (2) Use and Copying of Print Materials, (3) Performance and Copying of Video Programs, (4) Performance and Copying of Music (sheet music) and Sound Recordings, (5) Use and Copying of Computer Programs, (6) Copyright Responsibilities, and (7) Copyright Policy Violation Penalties. It is strongly suggested that this manual also be reviewed by an educational copyright consultant to assure that its contents are in agreement with the copyright law and related documents. A list of education copyright consultants appears in Appendix IV. The copyright manual should be reviewed biennially to assure that changes in the law, court opinions, new licensing and permission practices are reflected in the manual.

3. Name a Copyright Officer For the Institution.

An individual should be named and given specific written responsibilities for implementing and monitoring the copyright policy. As stated previously, this person should be someone with authority who can speak for the administration. He or she should not be considered a police officer, but as an information specialist. The placement of copyright liability on each employee should eliminate the need for the institution to police its employees.

4. Disseminate the Copyright Policy and Copyright Manual to Employees.

Distribute copies of the Board/Trustees copyright policy and the copyright manual to all teachers, faculty, and staff who may have need to use copying equipment as a part of their job responsibility. Workshops should then be scheduled to inform and discuss the copyright policy and copyright manual with employees to increase their awareness to the copyright law and their responsibilities. They should be informed of what they can and cannot do under the insitution's copyright policy and copyright manual. Copying responsibility and liability should be addressed as well as penalties. Attendance at the initial workshops should be kept small (under thirty) to facilitate discussion. Special workshops should be provided for administrators, librarians, media specialists, printing supervisors, etc. Institutions should provide longer or more frequent training programs for these individuals as they may have greater responsibility for interpreting or applying the institutional copyright policy and copyright manual.

The copyright policy and copyright manual should be reviewed yearly with employees to retain employee awareness and to upgrade changes. If an educational copyright consultant has been involved in reviewing the copyright manual, it may be advisable to have him or her make the initial presentation to the faculty and conduct the specialized workshops.

5. **Display Warning Notices on Copying Equipment.**

Appropriate notices must be placed on or near each piece of copying equipment to remind users of their copyright responsibility. Three types of notices must be implemented with the language of one mandated by the copyright law and two suggested by the American Library Association and most copyright consultants. Each notice has been discussed previously and the appropriate warning notices are exhibited in Appendix III.

SUMMARY

To implement an institution's copyright policy the following steps should be followed:

1. Develop a copyright policy in accordance with the copyright law.

2. Develop a copyright manual which will explain the institution's copyright policy to employees.

3. Name a copyright officer for the institution who will be responsible for implementing and monitoring the copyright policy and training employees.

4. Place appropriate copyright warning notices on or near all copying equipment within the institution.

5. Disseminate the copyright policy and copyright manual to the institution's employees, and implement a copyright training program.

CHAPTER IV:

RECEPTION AND USE OF TELEVISION PROGRAMS TRANSMITTED BY SATELLITE

The reception, recording and use of television programming from satellites by earth stations is becoming widespread today. During the past five years the size and cost of backyard satellite "dish" antennas has become relatively inexpensive ranging in cost from $1000 to $30,000 depending upon the quality desired. Communication satellites are positioned 22,300 miles above the equator where they maintain a stationary orbiting position above the earth. Programs are transmitted to these orbiting stations where the signals are returned to the earth and intercepted by "dish" antennas, tuned and converted to signals used by the standard television receiver. There are presently twenty-three satellites serving the United States, with 140 television program sources available to "dish" owners. Another nine program services are planned for satellite distribution soon, with some offering twenty-four-hours-per-day programming.

The existing satellites and their program sources are conveniently listed and summarized in *SAT Guide: Cable Satellite Magazine*, July, 1985 and *The Home Satellite State of the Industry Report*, February, 1986 (See Appendix II-E). Of the 118 program sources listed in those directories, all indicated their programs are available on a subscription basis for secondary transmission (i.e., cable television, hotels, motels, etc.).

15

Subscription practices vary. Twenty-four program sources are free, but most charge a monthly fee ranging from a few cents to ten dollars per-week, per subscriber/viewer. Some program sources require the purchase or lease of a decoder. Nine of the free program sources carry religious programs.

The legality of intercepting these programs directly from satellites and using them in educational institutions is a complex and difficult issue. The Communication Act of 1934, Title 47, *United States Code*, Section 605, "Unauthorized Publication or Use of Communication." states:

> [N]o person receiving, assisting in receiving, transmitting, or assisting in transmitting, any interstate or foreign communication by wire or radio shall divulge or publish the existence, contents, substance, purport, effect, or meaning thereof, except through authorized channels or reception...

Section 605 continues by providing the following exceptions:

> This section shall not apply to the receiving, divulging, publishing, or utilizing the contents of any radio communication which is transmitted by any station for the use of the general public, which relates to ships, aircraft, vehicles, or persons in distress, or which is transmitted by an amateur radio station operator or by a citizen band radio operator.

It would appear that this statement would make it a violation to intercept and use programming from satellites in educational institutions as well as most other places not specifically identified and exempted within the Communications Act, unless the programs are specifically transmitted "for the general public."

In October, 1984, this Act was amended by Public Law 98-549, Sect. 705, to authorize the reception of satellite signals **within the home**. Section 705 (old Section 605), "Unauthorized Reception of Certain Communications" is amended by inserting "(a)" before the above section (old Section 605) and adding a new section as follows:

"(b) The provisions of subsection (a) shall not apply to the interception or receipt by an individual, or the assisting (including the manufacture or sale) or such interception or receipt, of any satellite cable programming for private viewing if:

(1)   the programming involved is not encrypted;

and

(2) A. a marketing system is not established under which

(i) an agent or agents have been lawfully
designated for the purpose of authorizing private viewing by individuals, and

(ii) such authorization is available to the individual involved from the appropriate agent or agents; or

B. a marketing system described in subparagraph (A) is established and the individuals receiving such programming have obtained authorization for private viewing under that system."

Again, while this classification authorizes (under conditions of Sect. 705(b)) reception of satellite programs, **within the home**, one cannot generalize and assume it would be legal to do the same in educational institutions. A parallel application is the *Sony Corporation et al.* v. *Universal City Studios et al.* (the "Betamax Case") where the Supreme Court ruled that home use of television programs recorded in the home and used in the home for private viewing is not a violation of the Copyright Law. That decision was limited to recording and playback in the home and did not authorize recording programs and using them in the classroom. It would appear then that the Communication Act and the Section 705 amendment authorizing home reception does not authorize satellite reception within educational settings without appropriate agreements now available from many program sources.

We need then to look to the Copyright Act (Title 17, *United States Code*, Sect. 101, et seq.) for possible redress. However, a review of the copyright law does not look too promising for finding a legal avenue for considering satellite reception and use in schools legal. It would appear that nonprofit educational institutions **might** be able to build arguments for such use under the copyright law as follows:

1. The Copyright Law could possibly be applied to reception of Satellite programs under the definition of "transmit" (Sect. 101) as the definition includes "...by any device or process by which images and sounds are received..." It is generally understood that television programs (including those transmitted by satellite) meet the test of "fixed" as most are pre-recorded or recorded at the time of broadcast.

2. Using programs via satellites "live" without recording might not violate the "right of reproduction"(Sect. 106). Although it does not relate to the legal issues, this use would increase viewer count and could thereby possibly increase program ratings. However, it would be difficult to build an argument to authorize reception and use of pay TV programs or programs where a subscription system is in place.

3. Recording non-subscription satellite programs for "time shifting" purposes might be defensible and not violate the "right of reproduction" (Sect. 106).

The question is often asked if the fair use off-air recording guidelines apply for recording and using programs received from satellites. It would appear that these guidelines do not. The guidelines are limited to "broadcast programs" and broadcast programs are defined within those guidelines as "television programs transmitted by television stations for reception **by the general public without charge**." (Emphasis supplied) (Guideline 2, "Guidelines For Off Air Recording of Broadcast Programming For Educational Purposes," *Congressional Record*, October 14, 1981, p. E4751). The complete text of the guidelines appears in several policies included in Appendix II.

Given this short discussion on satellite use, it would appear that until Congress amends the law or some brave educational institution tests this issue in the courts, one should not use satellite programs in schools without appropriate agreements or without the advice and recommendations of the institution's attorney. The use restrictions from both the Communications Act and Copyright Act will have to be weighed very carefully before reception of television programs by satellite can be systematically used by educational institutions.

APPENDICES

I. Copyright Policy Examples

    Policy #1:   Birmingham Public Schools
                 Birmingham, Michigan

    Policy #2:   Granite School District
                 Salt Lake City, Utah

    Policy #3:   Central Washington University
                 Ellensburg, Washington

    Policy #4:   Madison Metropolitan School District
                 Madison, Wisconsin

    Policy #5:   Grossmont Union High School
                 La Mesa, California

    Policy #6:   Prince William Public Schools
                 Manassas, Virginia

    Policy #7:   International Council for Computers in Education
                 Eugene, Oregon

II. Television Satellite Information

    A. Communications Act of 1934, Title 47, *United States Code*, Section 605, Unauthorized Publication or Use of Communications.

    B. Amendment to the Communications Act, Public Law 98-549, October 30, 1984, Section 705 (replaces Section 605).

C. Videotaping Off Satellite: A Consultant's Letter to a Client.

D. Addresses of French and Spanish Language Satellite Programming.

E. Satellite Programming Directory.

F. Article Providing Legal Discussion of Reception of Programming From Satellites.

III. Copyright Warning Notices

A. Warning Notice Required At Employee-Operated Copy Center

B. Copyright Notice Required To Be Placed On All Copies Made By A Library Copy Center

C. Suggested Warning Notice To Be Posted At Unsupervised Copy Centers

D. Warning Label For Microcomputer Centers

IV. Educational Consultants Available To Review Copyright Policies

APPENDIX I

COPYRIGHT POLICY EXAMPLES

The following copyright policies included in this chapter are included as examples even though they sometimes contradict each other. The reader needs to study them carefully as to the appropriateness of each policy to one's institution. They are included here to provide ideas and background information to the reader regarding the development of a copyright policy and user copyright manual.

April 15, 1985

Dear   :

As you are well aware, the copyright issue is a large concern to educators and educational institutions at all levels. Copyright confusion still exists as insititutions attempt to develop policies which address the issue. As part of a research project, I am searching for copyright policies addressing the use of instructional resources that may be of value to others who are developing or improving their policies.

Your name has been provided to me through a previous questionnaire as a person who has developed an excellent copyright policy or is working within the confines of such a policy. I am interested in policies specific to the following levels or issues: (1) school district, (2) educational or intermediate school district (multi school), (3) college or university, and (4) policies addressing the use of television satellite signals for educational purposes.

Selected policies will be published in a forthcoming Copyright Policy publication to be published by Copyright Information Services with appropriate credit stated.

I would greatly appreciate receiving a copy of your policy or policies.

Thank you,

Sincerely,

Charles Vlcek, Director
Instructional Media Center

CV: lmn

APPENDIX I: COPYRIGHT POLICY EXAMPLES

COPYRIGHT POLICY #1

Birmingham Public Schools
1525 Covington
Birmingham, Michigan 48010

Courtesy:

Lucy Ainsley
Coordinator of Media Services
1525 Covington
Birmingham Public Schools
Birmingham, Michigan 48010

Copyright Laws

It is the intent of the Board of Education to adhere to the provisions of copyright laws.

Though there continues to be controversy regarding interpretation of copyright laws, this policy represents a sincere effort to operate legally. The board, therefore, directs the administration to provide district employees with guidelines that clearly discourage violation of copyright laws.

**Policy adopted: 12/6/83   Birmingham Public Schools
Birmingham, Michigan**

A new copyright law took effect in January 1978. Section 107 allows educators "fair use" based on four factors:

1. Purpose and character of use (instructional)
2. Nature of the work (various formats)
3. Amount of the work used (usually 10 percent limit)
4. Effect on potential market (sales)

Assuming the use is for classroom instruction, the next criteria applied is "nature of the work." The guidelines below explain what is permissible for each format. The amount of the work legally available under "fair use" varies with the format. Generally, copying should not exceed 10 percent of the total work nor excerpt the creative "essence" of the work (e.g., The two-minute time-lapse metamorphosis scene from "The Monarch Butterfly" is the essence of this film).

I. Printed Materials

A. Permitted
1. Single copies at the request of an individual teacher of
   a. a chapter of a book
   b. an article from a magazine or newspaper
   c. a short story, short essay or short poem whether or not from a collective work
   d. a chart, graph, diagram, drawing, cartoon or picture from a book, magazine or newspaper.

2. Multiple copies at the request of a teacher for classroom use (not to exceed one copy per pupil in a course) of
   a. a complete poem if less than 250 words
   b. an excerpt from a longer poem, but not to exceed 250 words

    c. a complete article, story or essay of less than 2,500 words
    d. an excerpt from a larger printed work not to exceed 10 percent of the whole or 1,000 words, whichever is less
    e. one chart, graph, diagram, cartoon or picture per book or magazine issue.

All preceding copying must bear the copyright notice.

B. Prohibited
1. Copying more than one work or two excerpts from a single author during one class term.
2. Copying more than three works from a collective work or periodical volume during one class term.
3. More than nine sets of multiple copies for distribution to students in one class term.
4. Copying used to create or replace or substitute for anthologies or collective works.
5. Copying of "consumable" works such as workbooks, standardized tests, answer sheets, etc.

Note: These prohibitions do not apply to current news magazines and newspapers.

II. Sheet and Recorded Music

A. Permitted
1. Emergency copies for an imminent performance are permitted, provided they are replacing purchased copies and replacement is planned.
2. Multiple copies (one per pupil) of excerpts not constituting an entire performance unit or more than 10 percent of the total work may be made for academic purposes other than performances.
3. Purchased sheet music may be edited or simplified provided the character of the work isn't distorted or lyrics added or altered.
4. A single copy of a recorded performance by students may be retained by the institution or individual teacher for evaluation or rehearsal purposes.
5. A single copy of recordings of copyrighted music owned by the institution for constructing exercises or examinations and retained for same.

B. Prohibited
1. Copying to replace or substitute for anthologies or collections.
2. Copying from works intended to be "consumable."
3. Copying for purpose of performance except for #A. 1. permitted.
4. Copying to substitute for purchase of music.
5. Copying without inclusion of copyright notice on the copy.

III. Audiovisual Works

A. Permitted
1. Creating a slide or overhead transparency series from multiple sources as long as creation does not exceed 10 percent of photographs in one source (book, magazine, filmstrip, etc.) unless the source forbids photographic reproduction.
2. Creating a single overhead transparency from a single page of a "consumable" workbook.
3. Reproducing selected slides from a series if reproduction does not exceed 10 percent of total nor excerpting "the essence."
4. Excerpting sections of a film for a local videotape (not to be shown over cable) if excerpting does not exceed 10 percent of the total nor "the essence" of the work.
5. Stories or literary excerpts may be narrated on tape and duplicated, as long as similar material is not available for sale.

B. Prohibited

1. Duplication of tapes unless reproduction rights were given at time of purchase.
2. Reproduction of musical works or conversion to another format (e.g., record to tape).
3. Reproduction of commercial "ditto masters," individually or in sets (including multimedia kits), if available for sale separately.
4. Reproduction of any AV work in its entirety.
5. Conversion of one media format to another (e.g., film to videotape) unless permission is secured.

IV. Computer Software

A. Permitted
1. New copies created as an essential step in the utilization of the computer program in conjunction with a machine that is used in no other manner.
2. New copies made for archival purposes only to be held in case the working copy is destroyed or no longer functions.

B. Prohibited
1. Creation of any new copies of copyrighted programs for any purpose other than the two permited above.
2. Creation of new copies while using a disk-sharing system.

V. Off-Air Recording

A. Permitted
1. A broadcast program may be recorded off-air simultaneously with transmission and retained by a nonprofit educational institution for

45 calendar days after date of recording.

2. Off-air recordings may be used once by individual teachers for relevant classroom activities and once for necessary reinforcement during the first 10 consecutive school days after recording.

3. After the first 10 school days, recordings may be used up to the end of the 45-day retention period for teacher evaluation purposes only (e.g., to determine if the program should be purchased for the curriculum).

4. Such recordings may be made only at the request of and used by individual teachers. No broadcast program may be recorded more than once for the same teacher.

5. Such recordings need not be used in their entirety but may not be altered or edited and must include the copyright notice on the program as recorded.

B. Prohibited
   1. Off-air recording in anticipation of teacher requests.
   2. Using the recording for instruction after the 10-day use period.
   3. Holding the recording for weeks or indefinitely because
      a. units needing the program concepts aren't taught within the 10-day use period
      b. an interruption or technical problems delayed its use
      c. another teacher wishes to use it...or any other supposed "legitimate" educational reason.

On occasion, a special notice is provided with some materials specifically prohibiting reproduction of any kind. Permission to use any part of such works must be secured in writing from the author or producer.

In no case shall any district employee or student use district equipment for duplication which would prevent or circumvent sale of copyrighted materials.

Regulation submitted for Board review: 12/6/83
Birmingham Public Schools
Birmingham, Michigan

APPENDIX I: COPYRIGHT POLICY EXAMPLES

COPYRIGHT POLICY #2

Granite School District
340 East 3545 South
Salt Lake City, Utah 84115

Courtesy:

Dr. Donald Hess
Media Center
Granite School District
Salt Lake City, Utah 84115

January 3, 1984

ADMINISTRATIVE MEMORANDUM NUMBER FORTY-EIGHT
COPYRIGHT REVISION ACT - TITLE 17 USC

The Granite School District is commited to observance of the Federal Copyright Laws.

It is the responsibility of the Office of Instructional Services to keep district personnel advised on the current status so that all district personnel may perform their duties within the intent of the law. Those employees in violation of Federal Copyright Laws and district policies relative to same will be held responsible.

See attachments #1 and #2. (These attachments are subject to annual revision.)

John Reed Call
Superintendent

mk
Attachments

Attachment #1 - Revised November 1983

GUIDELINES FOR SCHOOL USE OF COPYRIGHTED MATERIALS

Please note the following information which has been received from the Office of the State Superintendent of Public Instruction.

After many years of work on the part of thousands of individuals and hundreds of organizations, a new law became effective January 1, 1978, and will directly affect every educator and student in the country.

The following guidelines are based on the new law regarding the fair use of copyrighted materials. Keep in mind that the guidelines are not legal opinions. The law has many complex and untested areas in it. The courts will have to decide the final interpretation on these points. However, the guidelines are the product of a study by a committee established by the State Education Agency of the law and the best legal opinions available at this time. We believe they can serve as guides until legal action more clearly determines the provisions of the law. They do not cover all of the law, but rather select areas dealing closely with educational use.

It is recommended that a sign similar to the following be placed over each copying machine to protect media coordinators and school administrators from any infringement liability.

Making a Copy Without Proper Clearance May Invoke the Copyright Law

[Section 108 (f) (1) (2)] With Subsequent Penalties.

Without specific written permission of the copyright owner or broadcast station, an educator or student should comply with the following:

I. Print Media:

Permissible
A. Make a single copy for use in teaching or learning of:
1. a chapter from a book.
2. an article from a newspaper or periodical.
3. a short story, essay, or poem.
4. a chart, graph, diagram, drawing, cartoon, or picture.

B. Make multiple copies (one to a student) for classroom use only of:
1. a complete poem of less than 250 words.
2. an excerpt of not more than 250 words from a longer poem.
3. a complete article, story, or essay, if less than 2500 words and not a "special work".
4. an excerpt of not more than two pages but not more than 10% of a "special work". A special work is defined as works of less than 2500 words in the form of poetry, prose or poetic prose with accompanying illustrations intended primarily for children.

Not Permissible
A. Copy "consumable works".

B. Make multiple copies:
   1. for another teacher in the same school.
   2. of work from the same author more than once each term.
   3. from the same collection or issue more than three times each term.
   4. as a substitute for an anthology.
   5. of works intended to be consumed during the course of study, such as workbooks, standardized tests, test booklets, and answer sheets.

II. Non-Print Media
Permissible
A. Prepare an audio report on a new travel book in the school media center and use a copyrighted musical composition as background music.
B. Use an opaque projector to enlarge a map from a text or library book.
C. Use a film chain device to transmit a motion picture to classrooms within the one building, provided both the transmitting and receiving equipment is in the same building.
D. Make an overhead transparency of one page of a workbook or a text in order to demonstrate to the students how to proceed with an assignment.
E. Use a currently popular song as background music for a slide program produced as a class project.
F. Record a single copy of musical performances by students for evaluation or rehearsal purposes. (May be retained.)
G. Make a single copy of a sound recording (tape, disc, or cassette) of copyrighted music from those owned by the individual teacher or the district for the purpose of constructing aural exercises or examinations. (May be retained.)

Not Permissible
A. Make a videocassette copy of a 16mm educational film even though the school district has purchased the film.
B. Salvage useful frames from a discarded filmstrip to use for personal purposes.
C. Video-tape a preview print of a 16mm educational film.
D. Use a film chain to transmit a 16mm educational film to every school in the district or between different buildings on the same campus.
E. Make multiple cassette copies of classical music albums in their entirety even if the albums are not available in cassette form.
F. Copy various musical selections from radio or recorded programs onto audio tape in order to illustrate the forms of certain kinds of musical composition.
G. Tape the audio portion of a televised documentary for later playback.
H. Make a copy of audio records on tapes to use as masters if the circulation copies are damaged.

III. Computer Programs (software): Guidelines for School Use of Copyrighted Computer Programs:

Definition (as amended to Section 101 of Title 17 USC): *"A 'computer program' is a set of statements or instructions to be used directly or indirectly in a computer in order to bring about a certain result."*

Permissible

A. Section 117 of Title 17 USC allows the educational user to make a back-up copy of legally obtained computer programs. This revision of the law states *"...it is not an infringement for the **owner** of a copy of a computer program to make or authorize the making of another copy or adaptation of the computer program provided:*

B. *that such new copy or adaptation is created as an essential step in the utilization of the computer program in conjunction with a machine and that it is used in no other manner, **or***

C. *that such a new copy and adaptation is for archival purposes only and that all archival copies are destroyed in the event that continued possession of the computer program should cease to be rightful."*

Not Permissible

A. Illegal copies of copyrighted computer programs may not be made or used on school equipment; the same applies to the documentation which accompanies each computer program.

B. Computer programs purchased for use as "single-machine versions" may not be used to download a single program to a number of microcomputer terminals simultaneously (as in networking systems) unless so stipulated in a district-originated licensing agreement with the program producer.

C. Individual schools shall not be permitted to negotiate and sign licensing agreements for computer programs; this is a district-level responsibility of the Instructional Division.

IV. Guidelines for Off-Air Recording of Broadcast Programming for Educational Purposes

General Emphasis:

A. The federal off-air recording guidelines which permitted 10-day through 45-day retention rights have now been **rescinded** for channels 2, 4, 5, 7, 11 and 20 with the following exceptions:

B. Channel 7 (KUED); 9:00 A.M. through 3:30 P.M., Mondays through Fridays. This programming is identified in the latest UNIT "Instructional Television Course and Schedule" guide. The time length for program retentions is noted in the front of the UNIT Guide. These retention rights apply to Utah schools and districts only.

C. Contracted and special permission programming; may be retained for

30 days and then erasure is mandatory.
1. CBS Television Network news broadcasts
2. CBS coverage of political conventions
3. CBS news conferences
4. CBS coverage of governmental hearings and unusual news happenings which occur at unscheduled times
5. Local newscasts from Channel 5; these may be retained for 7 days and then erasure is mandatory
D. Television programs purchased from commercial sources (Sec. 110.1, Title 17 US Code):
   1. Educational television programs procured through direct purchase, rental or lease from commercial outlets may be used in the non-profit educational institution as long as they are a part of "face-to-face" teaching activities. The use must be part of the instructional program and *cannot* be shown for recreation or entertainment purposes. Section 110.1 of the Copyright Revision Act exempts the classroom use of a lawfully manufactured and obtained copy of a motion picture from the public performance rights reserved to the copyright holder.
   2. The label on leased, rented, or purchased videocassette programming which reads "FOR HOME USE ONLY" does not limit the *legal* permitted use rights of the educational user.
   3. With respect to where a motion picture or videocassette may be shown, the term "classroom or similar place" is defined on page 82 of House Hearing Report 94-1476 to mean a place which is devoted to instruction and would include a studio, a workshop, a gymnasium, a training field, a library, the stage of an auditorium, or the auditorium itself, IF actually used as a classroom *FOR SYSTEMATIC INSTRUCTIONAL ACTIVITIES*.
   4. It should also be noted that any duplication or copying of a videocassette is not permitted. This would apply even to the making of an archival copy or transferring from one format to another.
   5. In view of the above four sections (Part "D" 1-4) the following procedures will be required:
      a. All video programming obtained from commercial sources through rental, lease or purchase must be cleared for classroom use through the principal's office (or designee) AND registered on the school's "Commercially Obtained Video Programs Log."
      b. Each professional staff member who elects to use commercially prepared video programming must also present the lease, rental or purchase *receipt* to the school principal or his/her designee in order to confirm that the video programming has been legally acquired, is definitely relevant to the teaching of specific curriculum and will be used only as a part of "face-to-face" teaching activities.

34

Summary

Question: *Why the invalidation of the "off-air" dubbing guidelines?*

Answer: In a final court ruling as of March 10, 1983, the federal judge of the United States District Court in New York declared:

"...that any temporary videotaping and playback in classrooms of copyrighted materials readily available by rental, lease, or license duplicating agreement is infringement and is NOT fair use".

In a further statement, this federal court ruled:

"...that when such agreements are provided, fair-use guidelines for off-air videotaping of educational materials are not applicable; they do not have the force of law." *

ATTACHMENT #2

Works Produced by Granite School District Employees
(Works for Hire, Section 201. Title 17 USC).

A. Discretionary grant programs administered by the Utah State Board of Education such as mineral lease funds or Title IV-C and ESEA Title I, permits that materials developed under such grants and for which a copyright is claimed, must be credited to the Utah State Board of Education with the Utah State Board of Education being the sole copyright registrant.

B. All original works written, composed and produced by Granite School District employees as part of an assigned task while under employment, shall be copyrighted **naming the Granite School District as the sole registrant.** Such produced materials shall be solely owned by the Granite School District, including and reserving the exclusive rights for displaying, performing, printing, reproducing and sales. (Section 106. Title 17 USC)

   1. **Administrative Approval:** All original materials produced by any of the personnel of the various divisions of the Granite School District which are to be considered for submission for copyright registration will first be submitted to the administration. Upon administrative approval, the Assistant Superintendent, Office of Instructional Services, will initiate copyright registration procedures.

---

*United States District Court, Western District of New York. EBEC, LCA and Time-Life vs. ten named defendants of the Erie County BOCES. Civ-77-560. March 10, 1983.

2. **Original Materials:** Original materials are defined as those which have been independently developed, written or otherwise produced, which have not previously been published nor produced in any format by any other person, agency or entity.
3. **Use of Other Copyrighted Materials in Granite District Productions:** No section nor sub-sections of previously copyrighted works (by other authors, producers, publishers, etc.) may be used in composite with Granite District copyrightable works without proper written clearances and permission(s) declarations (Section 118, (f),(g), Title 17 (USC).
4. **Duration of Copyright (Section 302, (c), Title 17 USC):** In all works made for hire in the Granite School District, the copyright endures for a term of seventy-five years from the year of its first publication, or a term of one hundred years from the year of its creation, whichever expires first.
5. **Duration of Copyright -- Works created but not published or copyrighted before January 1, 1978. (Section 303. Title 17 USC):** Copyright in a work created before January 1, 1978 *but not* given over to public domain nor copyrighted, shall from January 1, 1978 subsist as copyrighted and shall endure for the term provided in Section 302 of the new law. In no case shall the term of copyright in such a work expire before December 31, 2002, and, if the work is published on or before December 31, 2002, the term of copyright protection shall not expire before December 31, 2027.
6. **Duration of Copyright -- Subsisting Copyrights:** Any works made for hire by the Granite School District prior to January 1, 1978 shall be considered as the property of the Granite School District with no attachments.

   Such works shall be considered as subsisting in copyright and this copyright shall endure for twenty-eight years from the date the works were originally produced.

   The Granite School District, as the sole proprietor of such copyright, shall be entitled to a renewal and extension of the copyright in such work for the further term of forty-seven years when application for such renewal and extension shall have been made to the Copyright Office and duly registered therein within *one-year prior* to the expiration of the original term of copyright. (Section 304. Title 17 USC).
7. **Infringement of Copyright:** Any employee who violates any of the exclusive rights of the copyright owner, owner being the Granite School District, as provided by Sections 106 through 118, is an infringer of the copyright (Section 501. Title 17 USC) and will be held responsible.

APPENDIX I: COPYRIGHT POLICY EXAMPLES

COPYRIGHT POLICY #3

Business Services and Contracts
Central Washington University
Ellensburg, Washington 98926

Courtesy:

Charles Vlcek
Instructional Media Center
Central Washington University
Ellensburg, Washington 98926

M E M O R A N D U M

TO: All Departments

FROM: U.A. Eberhart, Director
           Business Services and Contracts

DATE: September 24, 1984

SUBJECT: **Policy on Copying of Copyrighted Materials**

The enclosed policy statement was formally adopted by the CWU President's Advisory Council and approved as to form by the Assistant Attorney General.

The policy should be carefully studied by all employees of the University who either copy, or direct the copying of, any copyrighted works.

Please note especially the caution inherent in Article E, Page 3. of this document.

Appendix III provides a useful guideline on how to request permission to copy.

Appendix IV addresses the use of computer programs.

In addition to this policy, you may wish to refer again to the letter I sent to all departments January 30, 1978, on "Copyright Infringement Through the Use of Copying Machines." That letter contained six pages of questions and answers developed by the National Association of College and University Business Officers. The material was prepared as a guide to "fair use" under circumstances applicable to libraries and classrooms.

UAE/saa
Enclosure

CENTRAL WASHINGTON UNIVERSITY

**POLICY STATEMENT ON COPYING OF COPYRIGHTED
MATERIALS FOR CLASSROOM AND RESEARCH USE**

WHEREAS, in December, 1982, nine publishers commenced a lawsuit against New York University and nine members of the faculty (as well as an off-campus copy shop) alleging that the photocopying and distribution of certain course materials without the permission of the copyright owners of the materials, violated the Copyright Act (17 U.S.C. Sec. 101 et seq., 90 Stat. 2541 Pub. L. 94-553), and,

WHEREAS, it has become increasingly clear that the subject of copying for classroom and research purposes is of significant concern to the faculty and staff in matters such as when copying may be done without the consent of the copyright owner; when and how permission to copy should be obtained; how exposure to liability may be reduced; and under what circumstances the University will defend them against claims of copyright infringement arising out of copying for classroom and research use; and,

WHEREAS, the principles of the copyright law are intended to promote the creation, publication, and use of works of the intellect; and,

WHEREAS, these principles include both the exclusive rights of copyright owners to determine certain uses of their works (in not-for-profit as well as commercial contexts), and certain exceptions including the doctrine of "fair use"; and,

WHEREAS, under the copyright laws, certain copying of copyrighted works for educational purposes may take place without the permission of the copyright owner under the doctrine of "fair use" (presently set forth in Section 107 of the Copyright Act); and,

WHEREAS, the "fair use" principle is subject to limitations, but neither the statute nor judicial decisions give specific practical guidance on what copying falls within fair use; and,

NOW THEREFORE, to assist the faculty and staff in resolving these issues, and to facilitate compliance with the copyright laws, to achieve for faculty and staff greater certainty of procedure, to reduce risks of infringement or allegations thereof, and to maintain a desirable flexibility to accommodate specific needs, the following policies have been adopted by the University for use through June 30, 1985, and thereafter, unless modified. Requests for interpretations of this policy should be referred to the University's Director of Business Services and Contracts who may, as necessary, solicit legal advice from the office of the State Attorney General.

A. Certain copying of copyrighted works is permissible for educational purposes without permission of the copyright owner if the work is in the public domain. A work is considered to be in the public domain if:

1. It was published prior to January 1, 1978, without notice of copyright (required by the Act of 1909).

2. Its period of copyright protection has expired.

    a. For works published prior to January 1, 1978, copyright protection expires 28 years from the date it was secured, unless renewed.

    b. If renewed, copyright protection expires 75 years after the date protection was first secured.

    c. For works created after January 1, 1978, works are protected from the moment of creation, whether published or unpublished, and do not necessarily need to be registered or identified with a copyright notice (Section 302). However, a person who defends himself by proving that he innocently infringed a copyright in reliance upon the absence of a copyright notice incurs no liability for actual or statutory damages. Registration with the Register of Copyright is a prerequisite to bringing suit for infringement, and in the case of works published without the copyright notice, registration must occur within five years of the publication or copyright protection is lost.

B. The Guidelines set forth in Appendix I are to be used to determine whether or not the prior permission of the copyright owner is to be sought for photocopying for research and classroom use. To minimize intrusiveness and over-centralization, the responsibility for making this determination will continue to reside with the individual faculty or staff member. In making this determination, the faculty or staff member should carefully consider all sections of the attached Guidelines. If the proposed photocopying is not permitted under the Guidelines in Appendix I, permission to copy is to be sought. An explanation of how permissions may be sought and a procedure for furnishing to the administration information concerning the responses by copyright owners to requests for permission is set forth in Appendix III. After permission has been sought, copying should be undertaken only if permission has been granted, and in accordance with the terms of the permission, except as provided in paragraph D.

C. The Guidelines in Appendix II are to be used to determine whether or not television programs may or may not be recorded and/or retained. If the recording or retention of programs is not permitted under the guidelines, permission or licensing must be obtained. Programs may be recorded and/or retained only after permission or licensing has been obtained and in accordance with the terms of the permission and/or license.

40

The guidelines for determining if an off-air television use is permitted under "fair use" have been developed and agreed upon by a negotiating committee representing the producing and educational communities, and are now a part of the Congressional Record (Congressional Record, October 14, 1981). While the guidelines are the minimal requirements for fair use, additional uses may be permitted but only the courts can decide. Therefore, staying within the guidelines is the "safe" approach and any use beyond that must be approved by the office of the State Attorney General.

D. The doctrine of fair use may now or hereafter permit specific copying in certain situations, within limitations, beyond those specified in the Guidelines or those that might be agreed to by the copyright owner. In order to preserve the ability of individual faculty and staff members to utilize the doctrine of fair use in appropriate circumstances without incurring the risk of having personally to defend an action by a copyright owner who may disagree as to the limits of fair use, a faculty or staff member who has sought permission to copy and has not received such permission (or has received permission contingent upon conditions that the faculty or staff member considers inappropriate) may request a review of the matter by the University's Assistant Attorney General. If upon review the Assistant Attorney General determines that some or all of the proposed copying is permitted by the copyright law, he/she will so advise the faculty or staff member. In that event, should any such copying by the faculty member thereafter give rise to a claim of copyright infringement, the faculty or staff member may make a request to the Board of Trustees that the Attorney General be authorized to defend such claim or suit in accordance with the provisions of Chapter 28 B. 10.842 RCW.

E. In the absence of the determination and advice by the Assistant Attorney General referred to in paragraph D, or in the event that permission has not been first requested by the faculty or staff member as provided in paragraph B or C, no defense or indemnification by the University shall be provided to a faculty or staff member whose copying gives rise to a claim of copyright infringement.

GUIDELINES FOR PHOTOCOPYING

These Guidelines were negotiated by education, author, and publishing representatives in 1976 and were incorporated in the House of Representatives report accompanying the Copyright Act of 1976. The introductory explanation of the Guidelines in the House Report describes their relationship to the doctrine of fair use as follows:

Agreement on Guidelines for Classroom Copying
in Not-For-Profit Educational Institutions

With Respect to Books and Periodicals

The purpose of the following guidelines is to state the minimum standards of educational fair use under Section 107 of H.R. 2223. The parties agree that the conditions determining the extent of permissible copying for educational purposes may change in the future; that certain types of copying permitted under these guidelines may not be permissible in the future; and conversely that in the future other types of copying not permitted under these guidelines may be permissible under revised guidelines.

Moreover, the following statement of guidelines is not intended to limit the types of copying permitted under the standards of fair use under judicial decision and which are stated in Section 107 of the Copyright Revision Bill. There may be instances in which copying which does not fall within the guidelines stated below may nonetheless be permitted under the criteria for fair use.

I. SINGLE COPYING FOR TEACHERS:
   A single copy may be made of any of the following by or for a teacher at his or her individual request for his or her scholarly research or use in teaching or preparation to teach a class.

   A. A chapter from a book;
   B. An article from a periodical or newspaper;
   C. A short story, short essay, or short poem, whether or not from a collective work;
   D. A chart, graph, diagram, drawing, cartoon or picture from a book, periodical, or newspaper.

II. MULTIPLE COPIES FOR CLASSROOM USE:
    Multiple copies (not to exceed in any event more than one copy per pupil in a course) may be made by or for the teacher giving the course for classroom use or discussion, **provided that:**

    A. The copying meets the tests of brevity and spontaneity as defined below; **and**
    B. Meets the cumulative effect test as defined below; **and**
    C. Each copy includes a notice of copyright.

DEFINITIONS:

Brevity:
i. Poetry: (a) A complete poem if less than 250 words and if printed on not more than two pages, or (b) from a longer poem, an excerpt of not more than 250 words.
ii. Prose: (a) Either a complete article, story or essay of less than 2,500 words, or (b) an excerpt from any prose work of not more than 1,000 words or 10% of the work, whichever is less, but in any event a minimum of 500 words. [Each of the numerical limits stated in "i" and "ii" above

may be expanded to permit the completion of an unfinished line of a poem or of an unfinished prose paragraph.]
iii. Illustration: One chart, graph, diagram, drawing, cartoon or picture per book or per periodical issue.
iv. "Special" works: Certain works in poetry, prose or in "poetic prose" which often combine language with illustrations and which are intended sometimes for children and at other times for a more general audience fall short of 2,500 words in their entirety. Paragraph "ii" above notwithstanding such "special works" may not be reproduced in their entirety; however, an excerpt comprising not more than two of the published pages of such special work and containing not more than 10% of the words found in the text thereof, may be reproduced.

Spontaneity:
i. The copying is at the instance and inspiration of the individual teacher, and
ii. The inspiration and decision to use the work and the moment of its use for maximum teaching effectiveness are so close in time that it would be unreasonable to expect a timely reply to a request for permission.

Cumulative Effect:
i. The copying of the material is for only one course in the school in which the copies are made.
ii. Not more than one short poem, article, story, essay or two excerpts may be copied from the same author, nor more than three from the same collective work or periodical volume during one class term.
iii. There shall not be more than nine instances of such multiple copying for one course during one class term.
[The limitations stated in "ii" and "iii" above shall not apply to current news periodicals and newspapers and current news sections for other periodicals.]

III. PROHIBITIONS AS TO I AND II ABOVE:
Notwithstanding any of the above, the following shall be prohibited:

A. Copying shall not be used to create or replace or substitute for anthologies, compilations or collective works. Such replacement or substitution may occur whether copies of various works or excerpts therefrom are accumulated or are reproduced and used separately.
B. There shall be no copying of or from works intended to be "consumable" in the course of study or of teaching. These include workbooks, exercises, standardized tests and test booklets and answer sheets and like comsumable materials.
C. Copying shall not:
a. substitute for the purchase of books, publishers' reprints or periodicals;

b. be directed by higher authority;

c. be repeated with respect to the same item by the same teacher from term to term.

D. No charge shall be made to the student beyond the actual cost of the photocopying.

AGREED

March 19, 1976

AD HOC COMMITTEE ON COPYRIGHT LAW REVISION
By Sheldon Elliott Steinback

AUTHOR-PUBLISHER GROUP
AUTHORS LEAGUE OF AMERICA
By Irwin Karp, Counsel

ASSOCIATION OF AMERICAN PUBLISHERS, INC.
By Alexander C. Hoffman, Chairman Copyright Committee

APPENDIX II

GUIDELINES FOR OFF-AIR RECORDING OF BROADCAST PROGRAMMING FOR EDUCATIONAL PURPOSES
(Document: U.S. Congressional Record, October 14, 1981)

In March of 1979, Congressman Robert Kastenmeier, Chairman of the House Subcommittee on Courts, Civil Liberties, and Administration of Justice, appointed a Negotiating Committee consisting of representatives of educational organizations, copyright proprietors, and creative guilds and unions. The following guidelines reflect the Negotiating Committee's consensus as to the application of "fair use" to the recording, retention and use of television broadcast programs for educational purposes. They specify periods of retention and use of such off-air recordings in classrooms and similar places devoted to instruction and for home-bound instruction. The purpose of establishing these guidelines is to provide standards for both owners and users of copyrighted television programs.

1. The guidelines were developed to apply only to off-air recording by non-profit educational institutions.

2. A broadcast program may be recorded off-air simultaneously with broadcast transmission (including simultaneous cable re-transmission) and retained by a non-profit educational institution for a period not to exceed the first forty-five (45) consecutive calendar days after date of recording. Upon conclusion of such retention period, all off-air recordings must be erased or destroyed immediately. "Broadcast programs" are television programs transmitted by television stations for reception by the general public without charge.

3. Off-air recordings may be used once by individual teachers in the course of relevant teaching activities, and repeated once only when instructional reinforcement is necessary, in classrooms and similar places devoted to instruction within a single building, cluster or campus, as well as in the homes of students receiving formalized home instruction, during the first ten (10) consecutive school days in the forty-five (45) day calendar day retention period. "School days" are school session days--not counting weekends, holidays, vacations, examination periods, or other scheduled interruptions--within the forty-five (45) calendar day retention period.

4. Off-air recordings may be made only at the request of and used by individual teachers, and may not be regularly recorded in anticipation of requests. No broadcast program may be recorded off-air more than once at the request of the same teacher, regardless of the number of times the program may be broadcast.

5. A limited number of copies may be reproduced from each off-air recording to meet the legitimate needs of teachers under these guidelines. Each such additional copy shall be subject to all provisions governing the original recording.

6. After the first ten (10) consecutive school days, off-air recordings may be used up to the end of the forty-five (45) calendar day retention period only for teacher evaluation purposes, i.e., to determine whether or not to include the broadcast program in the teaching curriculum and may not be used in the recording institution for student exhibition or any other non-evaluation purpose without authorization.

7. Off-air recordings need not be used in their entirety, but the recorded programs may not be altered from their original content. Off-air recordings may not be physically or electronically combined or merged to constitute teaching anthologies or compilations.

8. All copies of off-air recordings must include the copyright notice on the broadcast program as recorded.

9. Educational institutions are expected to establish appropriate control procedures to maintain the integrity of these guidelines.

APPENDIX III

PERMISSIONS

A. How to Obtain Permission

When a proposed use of photocopied material requires a faculty or staff member to request permission, communication of complete and accurate information to the coypright owner will facilitate the request. The Association of American Publishers suggests that the following information be included to expedite the process.

1. Title, author and/ or editor, and edition of materials to be duplicated;
2. Exact material to be used, giving amount, page numbers, chapters and, if possible, a photocopy of the material;
3. Number of copies to be made;
4. Use to be made of duplicated materials;
5. Form of distribution (classroom, newsletter, etc.);
6. Whether or not the material is to be sold; and,
7. Type of reprint (ditto, offset, typeset).

The request (sample follows) should be sent, together with a self-addressed return envelope, to the permissions department of the publisher in question. If the address of the publisher does not appear at the front of the material, it may be obtained from **The Literary Workplace** (for books) or **Ulrich's International Periodicals** (for journals), both published by the R.R. Bowker Company. For purposes of proof, and to define the scope of the permission, it is important that the permission be in writing.

The process of considering permission requests requires time for the publisher to check the status and ownership of rights and related matters, and to evaluate the request. It is advisable, therefore, to allow sufficient lead time. In some instances the publisher may assess a fee for permission, which may be passed on to students who receive copies of the photocopied material.

B. Gathering Data on Responses to Requests for Permission to Photocopy

In order to help assess the effect of this Policy Statement upon the faculty and staff it will be useful for the administration to compile data on responses by copyright owners. Each member of the faculty and staff is therefore requested to forward a dated copy of each request for permission and a dated copy of each response to the Director of Business Services and Contracts, Central Washington University.

46

The following is a sample letter to a copyright owner (usually a publisher) requesting permission to copy:

Material Permissions Department
Hypothetical Book Company
500 East Avenue
Chicago, IL 60601

Dear Sir/Madam:

I would like permission to copy the following for use in my class next semester:

Title: Knowledge Is Good, Second Edition
Copyright: Hypothetical Book Co., 1965, 1971
Author: Frances Jones
Material to be duplicated: Chapter 10 (photocopy enclosed)
Number of copies: 50
Distribution: The material will be distributed to students in my class and they will pay only the cost of the photocopying.
Type of reprint: Photocopy
Use: The chapter will be used as supplementary teaching materials.

I have enclosed a self-addressed envelope for your convenience in replying to this request.

Sincerely,

Faculty or Staff Member

APPENDIX IV

1. University employees will be expected to adhere to the provisions of Public Law 96-517. Section 7(b) which amends Section 117 of Title 17 of the United States Code to allow for the making of a back-up copy of computer programs. That statute states, in part, "...it is not an infringement for the owner of a copy of a computer program to make or authorize the making of another copy or adaptation of that computer program provided:

   a. that such a new copy or adaptation is created as an essential step in the utilization of the computer program in conjunction with a machine and that it is used in no other manner, or

b. that such a new copy and adaptation is for archival purposes only and that all archival copies are destroyed in the event that continued possession of the computer program should cease to be rightful."

2. When software is to be used on a disk sharing system, efforts will be made to secure this software from copying.

3. Illegal copies of copyrighted programs may not be made or used on University equipment.

4. The legal or insurance protection of the University will not be extended to employees who violate copyright laws.

5. Nothing in this policy shall be deemed to preclude the University and the owner of any computer program or software product from entering into a separate agreement containing terms and conditions which are different from those described in this policy statement.

6. Nothing in this policy shall be deemed to apply to computer programs or software products which lie within the public domain.

APPENDIX I: COPYRIGHT POLICY EXAMPLES

COPYRIGHT POLICY #4

Madison Metropolitan School District
Madison, Wisconsin 53716

Courtesy:

Boyd Geer, AV Coordinator
Madison Public Schools
LaFollette High School
702 Pfaum Road
Madison, Wisconsin 53716

a guide to understanding the new

COPYRIGHT LAW

for the staff of Madison Metropolitan School District

March, 1978
prepared by Boyd Geer, IMC consultant
for District Copyright Committee

a message from the Superintendent:

The policy of the Madison Metropolitan School District must be to comply with the copyright law, Public Law 94-553, which amends in its entirety Title 17 of the United States Code. Compliance is the responsibility of each Madison Metropolitan School District staff member because it is you who will make the decision whether or not to push the button on the copy machine or recorder, and it will be your liability and possibly that of the district as well, if an infringement occurs. Therefore, it is your personal responsibility to become informed about how the law affects your work in the schools.

This will not be an easy task. The law is complicated and to understand it will require serious study. However, I believe it is in the best interests of our school system and the ethical responsibility of the teaching profession to diligently address the copyright issues with every effort to live within the law. Administrators, curriculum specialists, teachers, and media staff need to work together to develop reasonable practices that honestly seek to carry out both the letter and spirit of the law.

This guide has been prepared to provide staff members some basic information about the law and to summarize some of what may or may not be done. It gives directions on where to find more detailed information in the many national publications on the subject and on the process to follow within our school system. The starred items on the bibliography, available in every IMC, address specific situations and concerns.

Your support and cooperation is appreciated.

GENERAL INFORMATION

Background

"...to promote the progress of science and useful arts, by securing for limited times to authors and inventors the exclusive right to their respective writings and discoveries."

U.S. Constitution, Article I, Section 8. Based on this power, Congress passed the first copyright law in 1790. Four major revisions have been made, the latest having passed Congress in 1976 with an effective date of January 1, 1978. Advances in copying and duplicating technology were not anticipated in the previous law, passed in 1909, and revision was long overdue. The new law represents many years of effort to reach compromises between the interests of publishers and users. Our own Congressman, Robert Kastenmeier, who was a principal force in achieving passage, described it as legislation that "satisfies nobody completely but everybody can live with."

Copyright Defined

Copyright is a right granted by Congress to the author or originator of certain literary or artistic productions whereby his works are protected for a period of his lifetime, renewable for an additional 50 years, with the sole and exclusive privilege of multiplying copies of the same and publishing and selling them.

Copyright protection exists for original works of authorship fixed in any tangible medium of expression, now known or later developed, from which the works can be perceived, reproduced, or otherwise communicated, either directly or with the aid of a machine or device. Works of authorship include the following categories:

(1) literary works;
(2) musical works, including any accompanying words;
(3) dramatic works, including any accompanying music;
(4) pantomimes and choreographic works;
(5) pictorial, graphic, and sculpture works;
(6) motion pictures and other audiovisual works; and
(7) sound recordings.

A work is protected by the copyright law from the moment of its creation but the right cannot be enforced in the courts until the work is registered with the U.S. Copyright Office.

Fair Use

Many provisions of the law affect educational uses of copyrighted materials but the most generally applicable is Section 107 - *Limitations on Exclusive Rights: Fair Use.* Under the law, it is fair use to reproduce copyrighted materials for purposes of criticism, comment, news reporting, teaching (including multiple copies for classroom use), scholarship, or research. Four criteria will be applied in judging whether or not there has been an infringement:

(1) **The purpose and character of the use** - (commercial or educational)
(2) **The nature of the copyrighted work** - (textbook, workbook, tests, poetry, novel, music).
(3) **The amount and substantiality of the portion used** - (How much is being copied? How important is the copied portion to the entire work? How many copies are being made?)
(4) **The effect on the potential market for or value of the work.** - (Will the owner suffer unreasonable financial loss?)

Guidelines

The four criteria for determining fair use listed above were made very general. To aid in their interpretation, Congress urged representatives from interested groups of publishers and users to get together and agree on more specific guidelines. Three principal sets of guidelines resulted. They are:

(1) Guidelines and fair use photocopying of copyrighted print materials for educational purposes.
(2) Guidelines and fair use of copyrighted musical works in education.
(3) Guidelines for photocopying for interlibrary loans by libraries and archives.

These guidelines were not written into the law but rather they were accepted as part of the Congressional Committees reports and thus are included in the legislative history of the copyright act that courts will use in interpreting it's provisions.

An area left without specific guidelines at this time is audiovisual media. Representatives of copyright owners and users of audiovisual media have met and discussed the issue at length, but find it more difficult to reach agreement on specifics. They have agreed that the general principles of fair use can apply to audiovisual media and are continuing to search for ways to resolve the problems.

CLASSROOM TEACHERS

The guidelines for educational use of photocopying emphasize that in their application, three standards must be considered: **brevity, spontaneity, and cumulative effect.**

Brevity - The guidelines provide a quantitative measure of what might reasonably be considered minimum fair use. Different measures apply, depending on whether the work is a poem, prose, or an illustration.

Spontaneity - This means (a) that the copying is done at the instance and inspiration of the individual teacher, and (b) that the inspiration and decision to use the work and the moment of its use for maximum teaching effectiveness are so close in time that it would be unreasonable to expect a timely reply to a request for permission.

Cumulative Effect - This means that there is no intention to anthologize the reproduced materials, that the copying is for only one course in the school in which copies are made, that not more than one or two excerpts from the same author nor more than three from the same work during one term are involved, and that not more than nine instances of such multiple copying for one course during one term are anticipated.

Among the most frequently copied items are consumable materials (workbooks, exercises, standardized test booklets, and answer sheets). The guidelines state that any such copying, whether single or multiple copies, is **not** fair use and constitutes a definite infringement.

If a teacher wishes to copy materials in a situation that goes well beyond what the guidelines indicate as fair use, it is time to consider asking for permission. If indeed the material is educationally worthwhile, it should be worth the effort to seek permission for classroom use. Refer to the section in this guide on *Seeking Permission to Use Copyrighted Materials* to learn how this is done.

The following excerpt from *The New Copyright Law and Education* by Charles Gary is one of the clearest summaries available on practices for teachers.

WHAT TEACHERS MAY AND MAY NOT DO

The criteria for fair use of copyrighted works, together with the owner-user jointly developed guidelines, delimit the exclusive rights of copyright owners, especially in the area of reproduction for classroom use. Accordingly **a teacher may**:

1. Make a single copy of the following:
   - A chapter from a book
   - An article from a periodical or newspaper
   - A short story, short essay, or short poem
   - A chart, graph, diagram, drawing, cartoon, or picture from a book, periodical, or newspaper
   - A short excerpt (up to 10 percent) from a performable unit of music such as a song, movement, or section, for study purposes

2. Make multiple copies (not to exceed one per pupil) for classroom use of the following:
   - A complete poem if less than 250 words
   - A poetic excerpt if less than 250 words*
   - A prose excerpt of from 500 to 1,000 words*
   - One illustration (chart, diagram, graph, drawing, cartoon, or picture)

per book or periodical issue
- An excerpt of up to two pages of "special works" containing words and pictures
- Up to 10 percent of a performable unit of music (song, movement section) for academic purposes other than performance

3. Make a single recording of student performances for evaluation, rehearsal, or archival purposes.

4. Make a single recording of aural exercises or examination questions using excerpts from recorded copyrighted materials.

5. Make an emergency replacement copy to substitute for a purchased copy that is not available for an imminent musical performance.

The teacher **may also** display a school-owned (or personal) copy of a copyrighted work to those in the presence of the copy. Section 109-b of the law makes it clear that this includes casting an image of the copy on a screen through the use of an opaque projector. The law **does not** allow a teacher to make a transparancy (beyond the fair use limitations) because this involves making a copy, which is an exclusive right of the proprietor.

The guidelines also list some prohibitions that were agreed to be reasonable interpretations of the four fair use criteria. They specify that **teachers may not**:

1. Copy to make anthologies or compilations or to replace or substitute for them.
2. Copy from works intended to be consumable (workbooks, exercises, standardized test booklets, and answer sheets).
3. Copy to substitute for purchase of books, periodicals, music or recordings.
4. Copy on direction from higher authority (supervisor, coordinating teacher, or principal).**
5. Copy the same item from term to term without securing permission.
6. Utilize more than nine instances of multiple copying per course, per term.
7. Copy more than one short work or two excerpts from one author's works in any one term.
8. Employ a successful use of multiple copying developed by another teacher without securing permission from the copyright owner.**
9. Make copies of music or lyrics for performance of any kind in the classroom or outside of it, with the emergency exception noted above (No. 5).

---

*Numerical limits may be expanded to permit completion of a line of a poem or an unfinished prose paragraph.

**It was the thought of the members of Congress that the need to copy should result from the teachers' own spontaneous inspiration and the lack of time to get permission. The privilege that they granted exists to encourage creative teaching on the part of individuals and to allow them to catch the "teachable moment."

10. Copy protected materials without inclusion of a notice of copyright.
11. Charge students more than the actual cost of the authorized copies.†

Teachers should not ask other school staff members, such as librarians, audiovisual consultants or school aides, to do copying for them that is not fair use and for which no permission has been obtained. It may make these individuals liable for the infringement, along with the individual initiating the request.

Teachers should instruct students about the implications of copyright. Students frequently have occasion to use copying equipment, especially at the high school level, and should be aware of the provisions under fair use for copying material used for research and scholarship.

Under the penalties section of the law, individual teachers can be sued for infringement. However, there is an "innocent infringer" provision that protects the teacher who believed and had reasonable grounds for believing that the use of the copyrighted work was fair use. Refer to the section in this guide on *Penalties for Infringement* for further information.

MUSIC TEACHERS

The previous section that lists what teachers may and may not do includes the principal guidelines for fair use of copyrighted musical works. In addition, a booklet entitled, *The United States Copyright Law: A Guide for Music Educators*, has been issued jointly by several associations of music educators and music publishers. It contains a detailed explanation of copyright implications relating to musical works and has been provided for every music teacher. Additional copies for other staff members who might have occasion to use musical works are available from the Coordinator for Music and Art Education.

Standard forms to use in securing permission for use of copyrighted musical materials have been developed and are available from all music personnel and the Coordinator for Music and Art Education.

MEDIA SPECIALISTS

The guidelines for teachers explained previously also apply to media specialists. The word **teacher** is meant to include librarians and audiovisual consultants and other instructional specialists who work in consultation with teachers and are considered educators.

---

†From *The New Copyright Law and Education* by Charles L. Gary. (ERS Information Aid.) c)1977, Educational Research Service. Reproduced with permission from Educational Research Service, Inc.

Section 108 of the Copyright Law - *Limitations on exclusive rights: Reproduction by libraries and archives*, provides for library copying which parallels the fair use section, adding special provisions for preservation, security of collections, and interlibrary loans. To further interpret this section the Congressional report included *Guidelines for Interlibrary Loans* developed by the National Commission on New Technological Uses of Copyrighted Works (CONTU). Following is a summary from *The New Copyright and Education* of the provisions of Section 108 and the CONTU Guidelines.

Librarians may:

1. Honor requests for **single** copies of one article or another complete small portion of a periodical or book, or for an excerpt (10 percent of a performable unit of music) from a phonorecord, if (a) the copy is to be used only for private study, scholarship, or research, and (b) the request is not perceived to be part of a concerted effort to secure multiple reproduction.

2. Make **multiple** copies for a teacher if the item meets the tests of brevity, spontaneity, and cumulative effect under the fair use guidelines.

3. Reproduce and distribute a copy of an entire out-of-print work, if it has been established that no copy can be obtained at a fair price.

4. Make a limited number of off-the-air tape recordings of daily newscasts for distribution to scholars and researchers. (The term "off-the-air taping -- used in a number of spots in the law refers to making reproductions of the sounds, or pictures and sounds, from radio and TV broadcasts by recording devices.)

5. Copy an unpublished work in the library's collection, for preservation or security or for research use in another library open to the public.

6. Copy to preserve a deteriorating published work, if reasonable effort has not produced an unused copy at a fair price.

7. Participate in copying for interlibrary loan arrangements that do not involve such aggregate quantities as to substitute for subscription or purchase of a work.*

---

*Basically the "Guidelines" developed by the National Commission on New Technological Uses of Copyrighted Works permit: (1) making up to 5 copies a year for any one requesting library from those issues of a periodical published within 5 years of the request; (2) making up to 5 copies for any one requesting library of excerpts from any given book or other copyrighted work during its period of protection; and (3) supplying a copy of a periodical to which the requesting library subscribes or a book in the requesting library's collection, if these are not "reasonably available for use" and the provisions with respect to non-availability at a fair price have been met. (See the complete CONTU Guidelines, p. 44-45.)

Librarians may not:

1. Make copies for the members of a class if there is reason to suspect that all the students have been instructed to obtain copies individually.

2. Make copies on a systematic basis to avoid subscription or purchase at their own library or another.

3. Make copies of musical works, pictorial, graphic or sculptural works, motion pictures, or other audiovisual works (except daily news programs), unless it is for the purpose of preservation or security **or** in accordance with provisions dealing with fair use.

4. Copy without including a notice of copyright.*

Media specialists are not liable for unlawful copying done by teachers or students on their own as long as each machine displays a notice that the making of a copy may be subject to the copyright law. A sample of wording is shown at the back of this guide. Such signs will be provided by the Instructional Support Services.

As noted above, the law provides for videocopying of daily newscasts but this is only for use in research. The videotape may not be performed or shown to a class without gaining permission. However, in Wisconsin the Educational Communications Board, on behalf of schools, has gained permission from CBS News for the videocopying and use in classrooms of that network's newscast. This does not apply at this time to NBC or ABC.

Other than the above situation there are no guidelines for recording television or radio programs from commercial networks beyond the general provisions of fair use. Most recording being contemplated involves an entire program and that may not be fair use. There are court cases now pending that may decide the question before guidelines are devised. Media specialists and teachers engaging in such recording do so at their own risk. The best advice is to seek permission or cease recording.

Videocopying from public and instructional television is a different matter. Under a joint statement of policy, several public and instructional television agencies have granted schools permission to videocopy programs to be used in classrooms and to retain these rerecordings for a period of seven days. There are, however, certain programs and series that are excluded from the permission because of production or distribution rights restrictions. A list of these prohibited programs is published bi-monthly by PBS and includes such series as *Nova* and *National Geographic Specials*. A copy of this list will be distributed to all IMC's by ISS. Consult the AECT publication *Copyright and Educational Media* for more detailed information about

---

*From *The New Copyright Law and Education* by Charles L. Gary. (ERS Information Aid.) c)1977, Educational Research Service. Reproduced with permission from Educational Research Service, Inc.

the "Seven-Day School Rerecording Policy."

For many instructional programs now broadcast on WHA-TV and WERN-FM Radio, extended rerecording rights are allowed to schools beyond the seven day permission. Some programs may be retained for the school year and others for as long as the program remains on the broadcast schedule, which may be for several years. The publication entitled, *Parade of Programs* lists rerecording rights for each program. A copy of this booklet is distributed to each teacher at the beginning of the school year by the Southern Wisconsin Educatonal Communications Service (SWECS).

Both the AECT publication *Copyright and Educational Media: A Guide to Fair Use and Permission Procedures* and the NEA publication *The New Copyright Law: Questions Teachers and Librarians Ask* approach the explanation of the copyright law with the format of questions posed and answered. Many common situations that any media specialist might face are clarified. It is recommended that each media specialist become very familiar with these publications because he or she will be expected to be the first resource person when questions arise.

Many past copying practices common in our IMC's and at the district level may be in violation of the new copyright law. Although this is not condoned, it should not be a major concern right now. Rather, concentration should be placed on understanding the new law and following its guidelines henceforth.

One exception to this is the preservation of television programs on video-tape, which may violate both the previous and present laws. Since a great deal of money is involved in the loss of sales because of this practice, it might be well to erase those tapes for which no permission to copy has been secured.

The copying of records onto cassettes to allow for more compact shelving and to prevent loss appears to be a copyright infringement. New materials should either be ordered in the cassette format or permission to copy from record to cassette should be requested at the time the order is placed. ISS will not copy records onto cassettes unless permission has first been obtained.

The Educational Reference Library will no longer follow the practice of copying for general distribution such publications as *Epiegram* and *Education USA*. Under fair use copies of specific articles from journals may be requested, but not a copy of the entire publication.

ADMINISTRATORS

An excellent publication recommended to each administrator is *The New Copyright Law and Education* by Charles L. Gary. (*ERS Information Aid*)

Published by Educational Research Service, Inc., a nonprofit corporation,* it provides a comprehensive explanation of copyright, some suggestions for administrators to assure compliance, excerpts from the law, the guidelines mentioned previously, sample request for permission letters and sample forms.

Administrators are also referred to the previous sections which explain fair use and the guidelines as to what teachers and media specialists may or may not do. Administrators should be aware that fair use copying should result from the teacher's own spontaneous inspiration. The guidelines prohibit copying on the suggestion or direction from a higher authority, i.e., supervisor, learning coordinator, or principal. Thus copying that may be fair use for a teacher acting alone, would not be if an administrator becomes involved.

School administrators can assure compliance with the copyright law by following these suggestions:

(1) Lend authority to the assertion that compliance is in the best interest of the educational community.

(2) Provide information about the new law to all employees.
   a. Distribute this guide and encourage its study by all.
   b. See that the materials recommended in the bibliography are available to all staff.
   c. Hold inservice sessions for all teachers and include copyright information in the orientation of new staff.
   d. Display posters in duplicating centers and place warning signs on copying and recording machines.

(3) Consider copyright implications when preparing budgets.
   a. Copying an entire publication can be far more expensive than the purchase price, even when legal.
   b. Provide departments with sufficient budgets for materials in order to remove the temptation to copy. This is expecially important for consumable materials (workbooks, tests, answer sheets, etc.) which cannot legally be copied in any case.
   c. Create a fund to pay for royalties requested by publishers when teachers write for permission to use copyrighted materials.

(4) Assist teachers with forms and secretarial help in requesting permission from publishers to copy beyond fair use.

The two audiovisual presentations listed in the bibliography are recommended to administrators for use in staff inservice programs on the new

---

*Established and sponsored by the American Association of School Administrators, Council of Chief State School Officers, National Association of Elementary School Principals, National Association of Secondary School Principals and National School Public Relations Association.

copyright law.

Services at the district level that provide copying, recording, duplicating and printing should be conducted in accordance with the copyright law and will not be used to reproduce consumable materials such as tests, answer sheets and workbook sheets.

SEEKING PERMISSION TO USE COPYRIGHTED MATERIALS

Teachers should be aware that there are many uses they may make of copyrighted materials **beyond** those provided under fair use, if permission is granted first. There may be a charge or it may require no payment, provided ownership is recognized. Permission may be refused, but if the material is educationally worthwhile it should be worth the time to ask.

Determine ownership of a work from the title page or the reverse of it. Ask a librarian to help in finding addresses of publishers.

The letter of request should have the following information:

(1) Title, author and/or editor, and edition.
(2) Exact material to be used, giving amount, page numbers, chapters and, if possible, a photocopy of the material.
(3) Number of copies to be made.
(4) Use to be made of duplicated materials.
(5) Form of distribution (classroom, newsletter, etc.)
(6) Whether or not the material is to be sold.
(7) Type of reproduction (ditto, photocopy, slide, tape, etc.)

Other suggestions for letter of request:

(1) Include a blank at the end for the publisher to fill in whether or not permission is granted, conditions, authorized signature and date.
(2) Make three copies - one for your files and two to send to the publisher. One of these will be returned with publisher's decision indicated.
(3) Include a self-addressed, stamped return envelope.
(4) Don't ask for a blanket permission - it cannot, in most cases, be granted.
(5) Send by registered mail when response is crucial, such as for publications that will be sold or printed for distribution.

In the preparation of this booklet it was found that excellent summaries of what teachers and librarians may or may not do were included in the publication *The New Copyright Law and Education.* (ERS Information Aid.) Making multiple copies of the two pages involved and distributing them to a class would probably be fair use. But including them in this booklet with copies printed for each staff member in the district would certainly not be, especially since there was time to ask for permission. The letter used for requesting this permission is given as a sample at the end of this section. A sample form is also included.

Madison Metropolitan School District
Request for Permission to Use Copyrighted Materials

Date: _____

Permissions Department

_____

_____

_____

I would like permission to use:

Title _____ Author/Editor _____

Description _____

_____

Number of Copies _____

Use to be Made of Materials _____

_____

Distribution of Copies _____

_____

Will Material Be Sold?   YES   NO Charge for Viewing?   YES   NO

                        Circle   Circle

Type of Reproduction _____

Please sign one of the enclosed request forms and return it in the self-addressed stamped envelope.

Cordially yours,   Permission granted by _____

                                    Signature

_____ Conditions (if any) _____

_____ _____

_____ _____ Date _____

PENALTIES FOR INFRINGEMENT

Substantial penalties are provided for infringement of a copyright.

(1) An injunction to stop the infringement is most likely to be the first action.
(2) Payment of actual damages for financial loss suffered by the copyright owner may be required.
(3) Statutory damages, for which no actual damages need be proved, may be assessed. If the court determines there is an infringement, it must award between $250 and $10,000.

An exception to the statutory damages is made in the case of teachers provided the teacher believed and had reasonable grounds to believe that it was fair use. In this case the teacher may be found guilty but the damages do not have to be paid. This gives teachers some special consideration under the new law but it also requires that they be thoroughly familiar with what might be considered reasonable fair use practices.

Further information on penalties for infringement can be found in *The New Copyright Law and Education* by Charles L. Gary, (ERS Information Aid) from which the above information was taken.

FURTHER QUESTIONS

The following procedures for addressing copyright issues have been created to facilitate decisions on questions arising from the interpretation of the new law.

When a school staff person has a situation where copyright implications are unclear, questions should be directed first to the IMC or AV consultant. After discussion and examination of resource materials, if further clarification is necessary, district personnel should be contacted.

The educational reference librarian, Maryfaith Fox (226-6188) will receive general questions and seek answers to them from the appropriate staff. However, the following people will attempt to provide clarification in certain specific areas:

Music - Frank Lindl, Coordinator for Music (266-6015)
Instructional Materials - Suzy Bresnick, Text Librarian (266-6183)
Copying and Duplicating Audiovisual Materials - Mike Mattison, Instructional Support Services (266-6094)
Public Television Broadcasting - SWECS (266-8454)

Interpretations of special situations by the district will be publicized tc all staff through regular channels of communications such as the Staff New: and IMC bulletins.

APPENDIX I: COPYRIGHT POLICY EXAMPLES

COPYRIGHT POLICY #5

**Grossmont Union High School District
P.O. Box 1043
La Mesa, California 92041**

Courtesy:

**Ray L. Stansbury
Administrative Coordinator
Instructional Media Services
Grossmont Union High School
    School District
P.O. Box 1043
La Mesa, California 92041**

File: ECHC-R

REPRODUCTION AND USE OF COPYRIGHTED MATERIALS
(Non-print/Print)

The local unit chief administrator is responsible for the enforcement of the provisions of this regulation. He/she will identify an individual to act as a liaison person for staff information (inservice), control of approval process (written and verbal), and the maintenance of written records relative to the duplication and distribution of copyrighted materials.

Off-Air Video Taping

District Instructional Media Services operates an off-air video tape recording service for District schools. This service is available 24 hours a day, seven days a week, and includes all channels (except pay channels such as HBO, Showtime, Disney, etc.) that are carried on network or cable as well as instructional television with the San Diego County Office of Education (ITFS). The primary purpose of these procedures is to permit use of off-air video tape in face-to-face instruction and enable staff to preview instructionally related materials for possible acquisition through purchase, lease, rental, or free-loan agreements by the District. These guidelines enable teachers to replay television programs within a specified period of time.

To help prevent problems involving copyright violations on the part of the District or District employees, off-air taping of audio visual materials shall be accomplished under the following conditions and comply with the Governing Board Policy ECHC:

1. Any teacher desiring that an instructionally related program be taped by the District for classroom use shall complete a "Request For Off-Air/Video Taping" form (Exhibit ECHC-E). Such requests must be signed, which in effect is an agreement to abide by the provisions of this regulation. If a school elects to video tape at the local unit, a similar form must be used. An individual may use video programs taped at home as long as he/she complies with the policy and regulations adopted by the Governing Board regarding its use.

2. Unless otherwise authorized by the Associate Superintendent or his/her designee, all video tape recordings of network programs shall be erased no later than 45 days after the taping of the requested program. Instructional television programs broadcast over ITFS by the San Diego County Office of Education can be retained for the entire year (consult the County Instructional Television Guide for details).

3. Individuals who wish to retain programs beyond the 45 day period need to complete and return the preview evaluation portion of the "Request For Off-Air Video Taping" form to District Instructional Media Services

64

for each program video taped. District Instructional Media Services will be responsible for requesting permission to use or retain copyrighted television programs beyond the 45 day retention period. Video tapes of commercial programs may only be retained with written approval of appropriate copyright holders.

4. Copyright law and cable franchise agreements exclude the District from recording or using pay channels such as "Showtime", "HBO", "Disney", etc., for classroom instruction. This provision covers any program broadcast by pay channels and intercepted through the use of cable channels or a satellite dish. Exceptions may be authorized by the Associate Superintendent or his/her designee, and some "pay programs" may be available for legal acquisition.

5. Use of off-air recordings made from a satellite dish must conform to the 45 day retention period established for broadcast or cable programming.

6. Taped program shall not be exchanged with other schools in the Grossmont Union High School District or other school Districts without approval of the Associate Superintendent or his/her designee.

7. The taped program shall not be used for public or commercial viewing.

8. The taped program shall be used for the specific curriculum application for which the request was intended and no other curriculum application is authorized.

9. Published lists of authorized video tape libraries shall be prepared and maintained for each local site.

10. Video tape programs which fall under the State's Sex Education Codes 51550, 51820 and 51240 may only be used following the established parent notification and material review process.

11. Off-air recordings need not be used in their entirety, but the recorded programs may not be altered from their original content. Off-air recordings may not be physically or electroncially combined or merged to constitute teaching anthologies or compilations.

12. The principal of each school site is responsible for establishing practices which will enforce this policy at the school level. (See ECHE-E (2)).

13. The legal or insurance protection of the District will not be extended to employees who violate copyright laws. In the event said employee is found guilty of violating existing copyright law by administrative law judge, judge or jury, or a combination thereof, the employee will be required to remunerate the District in the event of loss due to litigation.

65

Letters of Request for Information to Major Networks or Producers

A request for information as to the availability of a television presentation, which has been determined to be of educational value for classroom use through teacher preview, shall be made to the appropriate major television network (e.g., NBC, ABC, CBS). Information requested will include the following (see Exhibit ECHS-E(1)):

1. Agency holding distribution rights to educational institutions

2. If and when program will be available to the educational market

3. Type of film or video format to be used

4. Procedure for purchase, rental, or lease agreement

Requests to Networks or Producers for Permission to Tape or Retain Copyrighted Works

Although some producers allow nonprofit organizations to reproduce their materials, they must first review the status of their copyright to determine whether or not they have the power to grant permission. Regardless of the standard policy a producer may have regarding the granting of duplication rights, each request requires a careful checking of the exact materials to be duplicated. Therefore, requests to producers for permission to duplicate copyrighted audio-visual materials shall include the following information:

1. Correct title of the material

2. Exact description of the material to be used (i.e., test, visuals, soundtrack, etc.)

3. Type of reproduction

4. Number of copies to be made

5. **Use to be made of reproduced materials:** If the material is a video cassette, specify whether the intended use involves single receiver playback or multiple receivers. If the intended use involves transmission of the material, specific information should be supplied as the method of transmission; whether radio or television, open or closed circuit. In such cases, many license agreements require that the number of students in the intended audience be stated.

Rental, Purchase, and Use of Video Tape

Copyright law and County Counsel opinion specify the following guidelines for the rental and purchase of video tapes. Due to the changing nature of the video industry these guidelines assure the District will remain in compliance with copyright and contract law provisions:

1. Use of feature length video tapes must be part of a systematic course of instruction and not for entertainment or recreation and their use must take place in a classroom or similar place devoted to instruction.

2. The purchase or rental of feature length or educational video tapes will be coordinated by the Associate Superintendent or his/her designee.

3. Use of video tapes must be made from legitimate copies.

4. Local schools may transmit video tapes over their closed circuit television systems for face-to-face instruction.

Computer Software Copyright Regulations

It is the intent of the Grossmont District to adhere to the provisions of the copyright laws in the area of microcomputer programs.

1. District employees will be expected to adhere to provisions of Public Law 96-517, Section 7 (b) which ammends Section 117 of Title 17 of the United States Code to allow for the making of a back-up copy of computer programs. This states that "...it is not an infringement for the owner of a copy of a computer program to make or authorize the making of another copy or adaptation of that computer program provided:

   a. that such a new copy or adaptation is created as an essential step in the utilization of the computer program in conjunction with a machine and that it is used in no other manner, or

   b. that such a new copy and adaptation is for archival purposes only and that all archival copies are destroyed in the event that continued possession of the entire program should cease to be rightful."

2. When copyrighted software is used on a disk sharing system, efforts will be made to secure this software from copying.

3. Illegal copies of copyrighted programs may not be made or used on school equipment.

4. The legal or insurance protection of the District will not be extended to employees who violate copyright laws. In the event said employee is found guilty of violating existing copyright law by administrative law judge, judge or jury, or a combination thereof, the employee will be required to remunerate the District in the event of loss due to litigation.

5. The Superintendent or his/her designees of this school District may sign District duplication rights agreements or licenses for software for schools in the District.

6. No employee of the District shall encourage or allow any student to surreptitiously or illegally duplicate computer software or access any data

base or electronic bulletin board.

7. No employee of the District shall surreptitiously or illegally access any data base or electronic bulletin board.

8. District Instructional Media Services is solely responsible for the duplication of all computer software licensed for District-wide use.

9. The legal, ethical, and practical problems caused by software piracy will be taught in all schools in the District.

10. The principal of each school site is responsible for establishing practices which will enforce this policy at the school level.

Printed Materials

No employee of the Grossmont Union High School District shall duplicate in any manner, any printed copyright material unless such duplication and its use falls within the boundaries of the "fair use" doctrine.

The Copyrights Act attempts to define "fair use" and establishes fixed limitations on duplication for schools and libraries. The law codifies four standards for determining fair use: (1) The purpose and character of the use including whether such use is of a commercial nature or for non-profit educational purposes; (2) the nature of the copyrighted work; (3) the amount and substantiality of the portion used in relation to the copyrighted work as a whole: and (4) the effect of the use upon the potential market for, or value of, the copyrighted work.

The principal shall determine where each copy machine is to be located and shall cause a copy of the "Printed Materials" section of this regulation to be posted in the immediate vicinity of each copy machine.

The following guidelines for duplication or printed copyright materials will be observed by all employees of the District:

1. **Books and Periodicals**
   a. A teacher or designee may make a single copy of any of the following for use in teaching or preparing to teach:

   (1) A chapter from a book
   (2) An article from a periodical or newspaper
   (3) A short story, short essay or short poem, whether or not from a collective work
   (4) A chart, graph, diagram, drawing, cartoon or picture from a book, periodical, or newspaper

   b. A teacher may make multiple copies (not to exceed more than one copy per pupil in a course) of any of the following:

68

(1) Poems or excerpts of poems of less than 250 words
(2) Complete articles, stories, or essays of less than 2500 words
(3) Prose excerpts of 1000 words or 10% of the work, whichever is less
(4) One chart, graph, drawing, etc., per book or periodical issue
(5) Excerpts from children's books containing up to 10% of the work
  in text

c. A teacher may **not** make multiple copies of the following:

(1) Works that have been copied for other courses in the school
(2) More than one work or two excerpts from one author in one term
(3) More than three works or excerpts from one anthology or periodical volume in one term
(4) Works more than nine times in one term

d. A teacher **may not** make copies of:

(1) Works to take the place of anthologies
(2) "Consumable" works such as work books and test booklets
(3) The same work from term to term

In each instance where multiple copies are allowed, each copy must include a notice of copyright.

2. **Music and Recordings**

As with guidelines for books and periodicals, duplicating copyrighted musical works is prohibited to replace collective works or "consumable" materials. In addition, music educators **may not** copy such works for purpose of performance or to substitute for the purchase of music.

A music educator **may** copy printed music in the following limited circumstances:

1. Emergency copying to replace purchased copies which are needed for a performance
2. Copying of excerpts of works for non-performance purposes, if they do not comprise performable units (e.g., a movement), and are less than 10% of the works
3. Copying of complete works if out of print or unavailable except in large works and used for teaching purposes

Schools are permitted to retain single copies of the following recordings:

1. Performances by students for evaluation or rehearsal purposes
2. Recordings made for the purpose of constructing aural exercises or examination

3. Reproduction of Works by Libraries

The Copyrights Act imposes major restrictions on reproduction of works by school libraries. Systematic duplication of multiple copies is forbidden by law with exception of the following carefully defined exceptions:

1. Inter-library loan arrangements are permitted, provided that copying is not done to substitute for subscriptions to or purchase of a work.

2. Libraries may make up to **six** copies of the following:
   a. A periodical article published within the last five years
   b. Excerpts from longer works

3. Libraries must keep detailed records of all inter-library loan requests.

4. Libraries may make **single** copies of articles or excerpts of records or longer works for students, provided the articles become the property of the student.

5. Libraries may make copies of unpublished works for preservation, published works to replace damaged copies, and out-of-print works which cannot be obtained at a fair price.

To avoid liability for copyright infringement on the part of the library or an employee as a result of unsupervised duplicating, libraries must display notices to the effect that making a copy may be subject to the copyright law.

4. Educational Performances and Displays

The Copyrights Act defines fair use of copyrighted material in classroom teaching and educational broadcasting. Teachers may use such material in "face-to-face" teaching activities. Such protection does not extend, however, to knowing use of unauthorized reproductions of works.

Nonprofit instructional broadcasts are given limited protection from infringement claims. An exemption is granted to works used in regular instructional programs for both closed circuit and open circuit in-school reception. In such situations, broadcasters need not obtain permission to perform non-dramatic literary or musical works, but must receive permission to act out dramas or musicals or show motion pictures and slide shows.

Issued: 3/6/78
Revised: 6/12/85

ECHC-E

REQUEST FOR OFF-AIR VIDEO TAPING

I, the undersigned, having requested the District Instructional Media Center to video tape the following program(s) within the parameters of the policy set forth by the Governing Board, March 6, 1978, am aware of said policy (see reverse side) and agree to accept responsibility for the use and erasure of this material to prevent any infringement of copyright law in lieu of expressed written approval of the copyright proprietor.

TITLE OF PROGRAM TO BE COPIED _____

DATE OF PROGRAM _____ DATE PROGRAM IS NEEDED _____

TIME OF PROGRAM _____ STATION OR CHANNEL _____

LENGTH OF PROGRAM _____

SPECIAL INSTRUCTIONS _____

_____

REQUESTOR'S NAME (please print) _____

SCHOOL _____ DEPARTMENT _____

SIGNATURE _____

PREVIEW AND EVALUATION

Would you recommend this material for purchase? _____ YES, High Priority

_____ YES, Low Priority

_____ NO

In what **specific** subject area(s) could this material be used? _____

_____

Is the material accurate and authentic? _____ YES _____ NO

This material could be used in _____ College Prep _____ Applied Arts _____ Remedial Classes

Do present District films adequately cover the subject areas? _____ YES _____ NO

Do you want the video tape of this program to be retained until information regarding the sale, lease, free loan, or rental of this material is obtained? _____ YES _____ NO

Overall evaluation (summary, use, etc.) AND/OR reasons for requesting retention of tape:

_____

_____

VIDEO TAPE STATUS-*OFFICE USE ONLY*

DATE: _____

_____ AVAILABLE   FORMAT: _____ 16mm _____ 3/4" _____ 1/2" VHS

PRICE _____

_____ May be retained indefinitely.

_____ May be kept on an indefinite basis, pending updated information on the program's future availability.

_____ Must be erased immediately

_____ May be kept permanently on a licensed basis.   REQUEST # _____

**(DISTRICT GUIDELINES FOR OFF-AIR VIDEO
TAPING ARE PRINTED ON THE BACK OF THIS FORM)**

DATE   ECHE-E(1)

NETWORK ADDRESS (ABC, NBC, CBS)
(Not Affiliate)

GREETING:

On *AIR DATE*, teachers within our district viewed the program *TITLE*. The quality of this program and potential education value for classroom use has prompted us to seek information concerning the agency holding distribution rights of this material to educational institutions. If this program is to be distributed to the educational market, we would appreciate knowing when it will be available, the format, the procedure for purchase, rental, or lease agreement, or whether an existing video tape of this program can be licensed.

While off-air video taping is a means of acquiring televised programs, we are requesting information for the legal acquistion of this program and hope we may hear from you concerning the above at your earliest convenience. Should you be unable to provide our district with the above information, please forward this request to the proper agency.

Sincerely,

Ray L. Stansbury
Administrator Coordinator
Instructional Media Services

RLS:jlb

GROSSMONT UNION HIGH SCHOOL DISTRICT
OFF-AIR VIDEO TAPE NOTICE

NAME _____ DATE _____

As a service to you, and in accordance with the district procedures (ECHC/ECHR-T--3/6/78), regarding off-air taping of copyrighted works, we are reminding you that the following video tape programs recorded for you on _____ must be erased:
(date)

_____

_____

Unless otherwise authorized by District Instructional Media Services, failure to erase these tapes within the 45 days allotted time period will place you in violation of federal off-air video tape guidelines and District policy, as well as jeopardize the school and District's ability to continue off-air video taping. This time period may be extended if permission is received from the copyright holder within the 45 day period.

Please return your tape(s) to your library/media specialist to be erased, or notification to him/her from your department chairman that the tape has been erased within the department.

Principal of School _____

GUHSD-6/80

APPENDIX I: COPYRIGHT POLICY EXAMPLES

COPYRIGHT POLICY #6

The County School Board
Prince William County
Prince William Public Schools
P.O. Box 389
Manassas, Virginia 22110

Courtesy:

Glenn C. Kessler
Supervisor of Instruction
Prince William County Public Schools
Manassas, Virginia 22110

SCHOOL BOARD GOVERNANCE AND OPERATONS

Copyright

The Prince William County School Board supports the provisions of the Copyright Law. The Superintendent shall prepare a regulation which provides necessary guidelines to assure that this law is adhered to. Appropriate notices will be posted at work sites and on all copy machines reminding employees of the Copyright Law.

Legal Reference:

17 U.S.C.A. #101, et. seq.

Adopted: June 15, 1983

THE COUNTY SCHOOL BOARD
PRINCE WILLIAM COUNTY, VIRGINIA

Regulation 157 - 1
SCHOOL BOARD GOVERNANCE AND
  OPERATIONS
January 10, 1984

SCHOOL BOARD GOVERNANCE & OPERATIONS

Copyrights

1. A notice of the Copyright Law shall be prominently displayed in close proximity to all copying devices, including photocopying machines, video and audio cassette recorders, and computers. The notice shall comply with the regulations of the Copyright Office and Section 5.5 of the *Manual of Copyright Information*, January 1984, Prince William County School Board.

2. *The Manual of Copyright Information* shall be distributed to all Policy Manual Holders and made available for review by employees upon their request. This *Manual* is to be used as general information only. It is not meant to replace the actual law governing copyrights. All employees who duplicate materials are held responsible for obeying the Copyright Law.

3. Persons approving requests for duplication of materials by the school division shall be responsible for certifying that the duplication of such materials is not in violation of the Copyright Law.

4. Where the duplication of copyrighted material requires approval by the owner of the copyright, such permission shall be in writing and kept on file.

The Division Superintendent is responsible for implementing this regulation.

Prince William County Public Schools

PRINCE WILLIAM COUNTY SCHOOL BOARD
MANUAL OF COPYRIGHT INFORMATION

January 1984

ALL EMPLOYEES PLEASE TAKE NOTE

This manual is provided for general information only. It is not meant to replace the actual law governing copyrights. Copies of the Federal Copyright Law (17 U.S.C. #101, **et seq.**), as well as other helpful information may be obtained from the Copyright Office, Library of Congress, Washington, D.C. 20559.

1. **Overview**

   1.1 Statutory Basis

   The Constitution and laws of the United States recognize the need to protect the property rights of authors, publishers, artists and others in books, music, films, computer programs and other creative works. At the same time the Congress and the Courts have recognized that the wide dissemination of information promotes progress in science and the arts, as well as protecting our fundamental freedoms.

1.2 Prince William County Policy

The Prince William County School Board supports the provisions of the Federal Copyright Law (17 U.S.C. #101, **et seq.**). Unlawful infringement of copyright will not be tolerated by the Board. It is the policy of the Board to take every action within its authority to assure that creative works are protected, that use of copyrighted material is in accordance with the appropriate law and regulations, and that creative works produced by the school administration, faculty, and student body are provided the same protection from misuse.

1.3 Management of Copyright Issues

The School Board recognizes the complexity of the copyright law, and the subjective nature of decisions required to be made in the school-related use of copyrighted materials. This Manual sets forth minimum standards of conduct, and if any staff or faculty member has questions concerning the use of copyrighted material, these questions shall be referred to the associate superintendent for instruction for review and determination.

2. **General Guidelines**

2.1 Compliance with Copyright Law

No agent or employee of the Prince William County Public Schools shall infringe upon the proprietary rights of another in creative works.

2.2 Permission

Except when not required pursuant to the Doctrine of Fair Use (Section 107 of 17 U.S. Code) and other statutory and judicial exemptions, the staff and faculty shall seek and obtain the permission of the copyright owner prior to making any use of copyrighted materials.

2.3 Notices

A notice of the copyright law shall be prominently displayed in close proximity to all copying devices, including photocopying machines, video and audio cassette recorders, and computers. The notice shall comply with the regulations of the Copyright Office and Section 5.5 of this Manual.

2.4 Responsibility for Compliance

The principal in each school and the superintendent or his designee for all schools and offices shall be responsible for enforcement of the requirements set forth in this Manual.

2.5 All copies made shall include the copyright notice as on the original.

3. **Copying for Teaching and Research**

   3.1 General Policy

   Teachers are **not** specifically exempted from the copyright law. However, the Congress has stated that

   > "The fair use of a copyrighted work....
   > is not an infringement of copyright."
   > (17 U.S.C. # 107)

   The Congress set forth four factors to be considered in determining fair use. These are
   1. The purpose and character of the use
   2. The nature of the copyrighted work
   3. The amount and substantiality of the work as a whole
   4. The effect of the use on the market or value of the work

   3.2 Research and Teacher Preparation

   Under the doctrine of fair use, teachers may routinely copy or have copied for research or preparation, a single copy of selected portions of books, newspapers, maps, etc. Generally, such copying should be limited to the following:

   1. One chapter or less from a book
   2. One article from a periodical or newspaper
   3. One short story, essay, or poem, whether or not from a collective work or compilation
   4. One chart, graph, diagram, cartoon or picture from a book, periodical or newspaper

   3.3 Classroom Use

   A. The copyright law explicitly recognizes that the doctrine of fair use extends to the making of multiple copies for classroom use. The doctrine applies primarily to the situation of a teacher who, acting individually and at his or her volition, makes one or more copies for students' temporary use. The doctrine does not extend to institutional copying, required or suggested by the school's administration, nor to copying of materials in order to implement a previously prepared lesson/teaching plan.

   B. Teachers shall include evidence of receipt of permission to copy materials planned to be used during the year with any lesson plan which calls for class use of copyrighted material, unless such material is or will be purchased from the publisher or other copyright holder.

C. The requirement of paragraph B shall not extend to the unscheduled but planned use of current articles from mass-circulation news periodicals.

D. In situations other than as set forth in paragraph B, teachers may copy (or have copied) multiple copies (not to exceed one copy per pupil in a course) for classroom use and discussion subject to the restriction in paragraph 3.5, provided that
1. The copying meets the tests of brevity and spontaneity as defined in Paragraph 3.4
2. The copying meets the cumulative effect test as defined in Paragraph 3.4 and
3. Each copy includes a notice of copyright

3.4 Definitions

A. Brevity
(i) Poetry:
    (a) A complete poem if less than 250 words and if printed on not more than two pages
    (b) From a longer poem, an excerpt of not more than 250 words.
(ii) Prose:
    (a) Either a complete article, story or essay of less than 2,500 words
    (b) An excerpt from any prose work of not more than 1,000 words or 10 percent of the work, whichever is less, but in any event, a minimum of 500 words

(Each of the numerical limits stated in (i) and (ii) above may be expanded to permit the completion of an unfinished line of a poem or of an unfinished prose paragraph.)

(iii) One chart, graph, diagram, drawing, cartoon or picture per book or per periodical issue. Such illustrations which are an integral part of an article, story, essay or poem which may otherwise be copied under subparagraphs (i) or (ii) above may be copied in connection with the copying of the article, story, essay or poem.
(iv) "Special Works": Certain works in poetry, prose or in "poetic prose" which often combine language with illustrations and which are intended sometimes for children and at other times for a more general audience fall short of 2,500 words in their entirety. Paragraph (ii) above notwithstanding, such "special works" may not be reproduced in their entirety; however, an excerpt comprising not more than two of the published pages of such special work and containing not more than 10 percent of the words found in the text thereof, may be reproduced.

B. Spontaneity
   (i) The copying is at the instance and inspiration of the individual teacher.
   (ii) The inspiration and decision to use the work and the moment of its use for maximum teaching effectiveness are so close in time that it would be unreasonable to expect a timely reply to a request for permission.

C. Cumulative Effect

   (i) The copying of the material is for only one course in the school in which the copies are made.

   (ii) Not more than one short poem, article, story, essay or two excerpts may be copied from the same author, nor more than three from the same collective work or periodical volume during one class term.

   (iii) There shall not be more than nine instances of such multiple copying for one course during one class term.

   (The limitations stated in (ii) and (iii) above shall not apply to current news periodicals and newspapers and current news sections of other periodicals.)

3.5 Prohibitions

   A. Notwithstanding any of the above, the following shall be prohibited:

      1. Copying shall not be used to create or to replace or substitute for anthologies, compilations or collective works. Such replacement or substitution may occur whether copies of various works or excerpts therefrom are accumulated or reproduced and used separately.

      2. There shall be no copying of or from works intended to be "consumable" in the course of study or of teaching. These include workbooks, exercises, standardized tests and test booklets and answer sheets and like consumable material.

      3. Copying shall not

         (i) Substitute for the purchase of books, publishers' reprints or periodicals.

         (ii) Be directed by higher authority.

         (iii) Be repeated with respect to the same item by the same teacher from term to term.

4. No charge shall be made to the student beyond the actual cost of the photocopying.

4. Copying for Administrative and Other Uses

4.1 General Policy

Although the Fair Use Doctrine as embodied in the Copyright Act (17 U.S.C. # 107) is not limited to teaching and research, its applicability in other areas is more limited. Every instance in which copies may be made cannot be foreseen. However, employees of the Prince William County Public School System shall generally reproduce copyrighted material only for personal use, and subject, at a minimum, to the provisions of Section 3 above.

4.2 Copying Technical and Professional Journals, Newsletters and Similar Publications

Administrative personnel and other employees, including teachers, shall not make single or multiple copies, for circulation to co-workers or colleagues, of all or any part of limited circulation periodicals which are intended to provide information of special interest to schools, school employees, or professional or technical specialties, unless prior permission has been obtained. The courts have consistently held that such copying is not fair use.

4.3 Copying Materials Concerning Prince William County Public Schools

A. Articles in newspapers or news periodicals specifically mentioning or concerning Prince William County Public Schools, or employees or students thereof may be copied for circulation and for archival purposes.

B. Articles as described in Paragraph A shall not be reproduced in other publications, unless prior permission has been obtained from the publisher.

5. Copying by and in Libraries

5.1 General

The requirements of Sections 3 and 4 of this Manual shall govern copying by library personnel and others, except as set forth in this section. Nothing in this section shall prohibit copying if prior approval is obtained from the copyright holder.

5.2 Reproduction for Preservation Purposes

A. One copy of any unpublished work already in the library collection may be made for preservation, security, or for deposit in another library.

B. One copy may be made of a published work for replacement of a work that is damaged, deteriorating, lost, or stolen, if there has been a determination made that an unused replacement cannot be obtained at a fair price. Such a determination shall be made by the chief librarian of the copying library, in writing.

5.3 Reproduction for Library Users

A. Library employees may make one copy of no more than one article or other contribution from a collection work or from a periodical, or no more than 10 of any other copyrighted work upon the request of a library user, as long as

   (i)   The copy becomes the property of the user.

   (ii) The librarian has no notice that the copy will be used for any purpose except private study, scholarship or research.

B. Library employees may copy all or substantial parts of a copyrighted work under the conditions stated in Paragraph 5.3(A) if a determination has been previously made that an unused copy cannot be obtained at a fair price. Such determination shall be made as provided in Paragraph 5.2(B).

5.4 Restrictions on Copying

A. Except as provided in Subparagraph B, libraries shall not copy musical works, pictures, graphic or sculptural works, motion pictures, videotapes or audiotapes except for the purposes stated in Paragraph 5.2.

B. Notwithstanding subparagraph 5.4(A), copies of pictorial or graphic works published as illustrations, diagrams, or similar adjuncts to works reproduced upon Paragraph 5.3 may be made as a part of the works reproduced in accordance with that paragraph.

C. Libraries shall not reproduce works in "machine-readable" language for storage in electronic or other information systems, unless prior approval from the copyright holder is obtained.

D. Notwithstanding anything to the contrary contained in this Manual, librarians shall not copy or allow others to copy any document in derogation of express contractual prohibitions against reproduction for any use or purpose.

5.5 Notices Required at Reproduction Facilities

A. A Display Warning of Copyright as set forth in Subparagraph B and complying with Subparagraph C shall be prominently displayed in such manner and location to be clearly visible, legible and comprehensible to a casual observer within the immediate vicinity of any device capable of reproducing copies of copyrighted works, including photocopiers, mimeograph machines, video cassette recorders, computers (with disk copying capabilities) and audiotape machines (with reproduction capabilities).

B. Notice

NOTICE WARNING CONCERNING COPYRIGHT RESTRICTIONS

The copyright law of the United States (Title 17, United States Code) governs the making of photocopies or other reproductions of copyrighted material.

Under certain conditions specified in the law, libraries and archives are authorized to furnish a photocopy or other reproduction. One of these specific conditions is that the photocopy or reproduction is not to be "used for any purpose other than private study, scholarship, or research." If a user makes a request for, or later uses, a photocopy or reproduction for purposes in excess of "fair use," that user may be liable for copyright infringement.

This institution reserves the right to refuse to accept a copying order if, in its judgement fulfillment of the order would involve violation of copyright law.

C. The Display Notice shall be printed on heavy paper or other durable material in type at least 18 points in size.

D. All school facilities accepting orders for reproduction shall include the language in subparagraph B on all order forms, plus the following statement: "This request complies with the Copyright Law and School Board Regulation 157-1 (and its accompanying manual), and (if applicable) a copy of the approval to reproduce copyrighted material is attached." The notice shall be printed within a box located prominently on the order form, either on the front side or immediately adjacent to the space calling for the name or signature of the person ordering the copies. The notice shall be printed in type size no smaller than that used throughout the form, and in no case shall the type be smaller than 8 points.

5.6 Recording and Copying Television and Radio Broadcasts

A. Librarians may record and copy for archival, research, or teaching purposes, news broadcasts, without prior permission.

B. Librarians shall not record or copy any other copyrighted audio-visual material, or allow others to do so, unless prior permission is obtained, except as is allowed under Section 8. Material which shall not be copied includes, but is not limited to, dramatic works, documentaries, regular non-news series, live performances, and educational programs.

6. Copying Musical Works

6.1 General

The Copyright Act gives copyright holders the exclusive right to

(i) Reproduce the copyrighted work.

(ii) Prepare derivative works based on the copyrighted work (including arrangements, lyrical adaptations of instrumental works, and simplified "student" versions), and

(iii) Perform the copyrighted work publicly.

While there are exemptions provided in the Act, and implemented in this Section, the general principle of exclusive right is applicable to use by schools.

In addition to the requirements of this Section, the provisions of all other Sections of this Manual shall be fully applicable to music instruction and other school activities involving music. The performance of musical and literary works is governed by Section 7 of this Manual.

6.2 Use of Music for Academic Purposes

A. For academic purposes other than performance, multiple copies of excerpts of works may be made, without permission, provided that the excerpts do not comprise a part of the whole which would constitute a performable unit such as a section, movement or aria, but in no case more than 10 percent of the whole work. The number of copies shall not exceed one copy per pupil.

B. Printed copies which have been purchased may be edited or simplified provided that the fundamental character of the work is not distorted or the lyrics, if any, altered or lyrics added if none exist.

C. A single copy of recordings of performances by students may be made for evaluation or rehearsal purposes and may be retained by the education institution or individual teacher.

D. Copies shall not be made to create, replace, or substitute for anthologies, compilations or collective works.

E. Copies of "consumable" works (including workbooks, exercises, standardized tests and answer sheets) shall not be made.

6.3 Research and Teacher Preparation

A. A single copy of an entire performable unit (section, movement, aria, etc.) that is (1) confirmed by the copyright proprietor to be out of print, or (2) unavailable except in a larger work, may be made by or for a teacher solely for the purpose of his or her scholarly research or in preparation to teach a class.

B. A single copy of a sound recording (such as a tape, disc or cassette) of copyrighted music may be made from sound recordings owned by an individual teacher for the purpose of constructing aural exercises or examinations and may be retained by the individual teacher. (This pertains only to the copyright of the music itself and not to any copyright which may exist in the sound recording.)

6.4 Other Exemptions from Copyright Requirements

Copies of music may be made for performance purposes without permission only in emergencies to replace purchased copies which are, for any reason, not available for an imminent performance. Such copies shall be replaced as soon as practicable.

7. **Performance of Musical Works**

7.1 General

Most performances of non-dramatic works by school orchestras, bands or choral groups are exempt from licensing requirements under Section 110 of the Copyright Act. Operas and musicals are treated in Section 9 of this Manual.

7.2 Educational Use

A. All performances of both dramatic and non-dramatic musical works in class are exempt from copyright requirements.

B. All broadcasts and transmissions of non-dramatic works for classroom or instructional use are exempt. However, the copyright owner's permission is required for transmission of dramatic works, such as operas or musicals.

7.3 Public Performances

Public performances of non-dramatic musical works are exempt from copyright requirements if

1. Any fees or admission charges are used for educational purposes

2. No performer, promoter or organizer is compensated (except by regular salary in the case of school employees)

3. No organization makes use of the performance for commercial advantage (i.e., performance by the high school band which is used in a commercial for a soft drink are not exempt).

7.4 Non-Exempt Performances

A. Except as provided in subparagraph (B) below, sponsoring organizations with direct or indirect commercial purposes which organize or arrange for a public performance by any Prince William performing group shall, as a part of the performance agreement, be required to be responsible for all performance royalties due, and shall arrange for permission for performance, recording and transmission rights.

B. Notwithstanding the requirements of subparagraph (A), prior permission is not required to perform musical works at parades, sports events, and student social events, not coming within the exemption provided by Paragraph 7.3, unless specific restrictions on such performances are set forth on the musical works.

8. **Recording and Transmission of Copyrighted Works: Display and Performance of Audiovisual Works**

8.1 General

A. The statutory balance between the rights of copyright holders and educational institutions creates a complex situation in which instructors and the school administration must carefully evaluate the purpose, use and medium of recording or transmission in order to determine the applicability of copyright requirements to taping performances as well as storage and later re-use.

B. For the purposes of this Manual, to "transmit" a performance is to communicate it by any device or process whereby images or sounds are received beyond the place from which they are sent. To "record" is to fix a series of images or sounds in any medium which can be used for later viewing or listening.

C. It is important to note that the law concerning "off-the-air" recording is presently unsettled. A group of trade and profes-

86

sional associations, working with the Copyright Office, has developed guidelines for such recording. These guidelines have been published in the *Congressional Record*, and republished in the WNVT publication *WNVT File 53*, but they **do not** have the force of law and have not been approved by Congress. Further, at least in one case, a Federal Judge has refused to allow a school system to operate under the guidelines. Accordingly, Prince William County Public Schools is not at this time accepting these guidelines; and teachers should not rely on them. The regulations provided in this Section shall be followed instead.

8.2   Recording Material Other Than Music "Off-the-Air" Without Prior Permission -- General Rule

Except for audiovisual news programs which are copied pursuant to Paragraph 5.6 (A), and except as allowed by Paragraph 8.4, copyrighted material broadcast by commercial/for-profit broadcasters shall not be copied or recorded in any form by any teacher or staff member, unless prior permission is obtained.

8.3   Recording Transmissions from WNVT

Prince William County Public Schools has arranged for certain re-recording rights with WNVT for programs in its schedule. The rights, restrictions and requirements involved vary from program to program and change over time. Guidance on use of WNVT programs is covered by the WNVT publication, WNVT *File 53*, and is updated by the monthly WNVT publication *53 Close-Up*. Where *File 53* states "standard re-record rights," instructors may record only as provided below.

8.4   Fair Use Recording Transmissions From Other Transmitters Without Permission

Individual teachers may record broadcast programs (including simultaneous cable retransmissions) for use in preparation and instruction, subject to the requirements of this Section. Broadcast programs are limited to programs transmitted for reception by the general public, without charge. Pay T.V. programs shall not be copied.

8.5   Use and Retention

Programs which have been recorded may be used only once in each class and may be retained for no more than ten (10) days after broadcast. After ten days, any copy or copies must be erased or destroyed.

8.6   Impetus for Copying

The decision to record a program shall be solely that of the individual teacher, shall comply with the test for spontaneity as set forth in Paragraph 3.4 (A), and shall meet the cumulative effect test stated in Paragraph 8.7.

8.7 Cumulative Effect

In any one school year, instructors shall use no more than the lesser of five (5) hours or nine different programs or program segments recorded without permission. In addition, not more than two (2) segments of the same program series shall be used.

8.8 Repetitive Use

No program may be recorded off-the-air more than once by or for the same teacher.

8.9 Copyright Notice

The copyright notice included in the original broadcast must be included in any copy made. The segment displaying the copyright must be displayed.

8.10 Editing Recorded Material

Programs need not be shown in their entirety, but recordings shall not be edited or altered in any way. Anthologies or compilations of programs shall not be produced, either by editing, recordings or by selective recording.

8.11 Recordkeeping

Each instructor shall maintain a record of recordings made pursuant to Paragraph 8.4 showing the date recorded, date(s) used and date erased. Persons recording programs for individual instructors shall maintain a record of such recordings, showing the requesting instructor, program title, date recorded, date returned and date erased.

8.12 Transmission

Programs recorded in accordance with either Paragraph 8.3 or Paragraph 8.4 shall not be transmitted by any means except through WNVT unless prior permission is obtained.

8.13 Use of Rented or Purchased Videotapes and Films

Unless purchased or rented under a license which specifically permits transmission, no videotape or film may be transmitted and all performances shall be solely for face-to-face instructional or training purposes. Provided, however, that closed-circuit transmission within a single building to one or more classrooms shall not be considered transmission for purposes of this paragraph.

9. Dramatic Works

9.1 General

Other than in face-to-face classroom use, most performances of copyrighted dramatic works by school groups are not exempt from copyright requirements. In most cases, the dramatic works will be obtained from publishers or others and performance agreements will be signed as a matter of course. However, the rights provided under the copyright law are such that guidelines are necessary.

9.2 Use of Dramatic Works

Other than in face-to-face classroom use, which is exempt from copyright restriction, dramatic works (including plays, operas, pantomimes, comedy "skits," and ballets) shall not be performed or recorded without permission of the copyright holder.

9.3 Dramatizations

The copyright law gives copyright owners the exclusive right to dramatize, adapt, arrange and perform their works. Accordingly, no copyrighted work(s) shall be used in any student or faculty dramatization sanctioned by Prince William County Public Schools or any division thereof which will be performed outside of the classroom unless prior permission is obtained from the copyright holder(s).

9.4 Scope of Permission

Persons seeking permission from copyright holders shall request the right to adapt, arrange, dramatize and perform the work(s) as required, and, in addition, if no extra cost is incurred, the right to record and transmit such performances for school-related non-commercial purposes.

9.5 Recordkeeping

School activities sponsoring, organizing or supervising performances for which permission has been obtained shall retain records of such permission and of royalties or other fees paid for a period of three (3) years after the final performance of the work.

10. Copying Computer Software and Data

10.1 General

Computer software is subject to copyright, whether it is in human or machine-readable format. Unauthorized copying can lead to civil and even criminal liability. As the use of computers has mushroomed, the issue of software "piracy" has become very important. Prince William County Public Schools will not tolerate illicit copying of valuable computer software by students, faculty or staff, any more than any other kind of theft.

10.2 Policy

Except for archival or operationally essential purposes allowed under Paragraphs 10.3 and 10.4, no copies of copyrighted computer programs in any format or media may be made without permission of the copyright holder.

10.3 Archival Copies

A reasonable number of copies of a computer program, not in excess of those allowed under the applicable license, may be made for archival purposes. Archival copies shall be stored in a secure place and shall not be used for operational purposes.

10.4 Copies Made in Computer Operations

Copies created as an essential step in the utilization of a computer program, and used in no other manner, may be made without permission.

10.5 Use of Data in Computer Systems

Copyrighted works, such as books, articles, poems, musical works and testing instruments, will not be input into automated information systems without permission, except to the extent that such works could be copied under Section 3.

11. **Obtaining Permission or Licenses**

11.1 General

Most copyright owners will grant permission for one-time use of parts of their works without charge, or upon payment of a minimal fee. However, repeated use or republication is often not allowed unless royalties are paid. These royalties are the legitimate compensation for the creative effort made by the author, lyricist, composer, artist, or other producer of copyrighted works. To avoid payment by unauthorized copying is theft, no different from stealing a book from a bookstore. While Prince William County Public Schools has a limited budget, it does not condone any violation of law simply because that violation saves the taxpayers' money. Accordingly, in every circumstance possible, prior permission shall be obtained for the use of copyrighted works.

11.2 Persons Responsible for Obtaining Permission

    A. The following persons shall be responsible for planned acquisition of prior permission to use copyrighted works.

Type of Work	Responsible Person
1. Complete books or other publications (including testing instruments)	Associate Superintendent for Instruction, or designee
2. Reprints of articles, stories, poems, etc. from larger works	Associate Superintendent for Instruction, or designee
3. Musical works (sheet music)	Supervisor of Music
4. Musical performing rights	Supervisor of Music
5. Films and videotapes (including off-the-air recording rights)	Supervisor of Instructional Computing & Educational Technology
6. Dramatic works (including performing rights)	Supervisor of Language Arts
7. Computer Software	Supervisor of Instructional Computing & Educational Technology

    B. Individual instructors may, in the alternative, directly arrange for permission with copyright holders.

11.3 Requests for Permission

    A. Wherever possible, requests for permission shall be in writing. All requests shall identify the user as the Prince William County Public Schools or the appropriate part thereof.

    B. If repeated use is contemplated, the request should normally so state. However, many publications will grant requests for small numbers of copies at no charge, but require payment if large numbers of copies will be made. The person responsible for requesting permission shall compare the costs of repeated requests to the royalties charged in determining whether to make a bulk request.

C. Requests by individual instructors placed with other school employees listed in Paragraph 11.2 shall include the following information.

1. Name of work for which permission is requested.

2. Work from which requested work is drawn, if the request is for less than the entire work (e.g., a single poem from a compilation).

3. Author, publisher or producer, and copyright holder, if known.

4. Date of publication, if known.

5. Numbers of copies/performances or other use.

6. Intended use.

7. Source of payment of royalties, if any.

11.4 Sources for Granting Permission

Permission to use most books, articles, and other printed matter, as well as dramatic works, should be requested directly from the copyright holder. While permission may be similarly obtained for most other works, it is possible in some cases to use one or more of the organizations (or similar ones) listed in Paragraph 11.5 to obtain "blanket" licenses for certain kinds of works. If permission is needed for many kinds of works, the use of these sources should be considered.

11.5 Organizations Granting Performance, Re-Recording or Other Licenses

A. Music

1. American Society of Composers, Authors, and Publishers, New York, New York

2. Broadcast Music, Inc., New York, New York

3. SESAC, Inc., New York, New York

B. Videotapes and Films

Many organizations have been organized to arrange for re-recording rights as well as rent or sell video programs and films One of the larger companies in this area is the Films, Inc. Television Licensing Center, in Wilmette, Ill. This organization grants "master" licenses for recording programs "off-the-air" and the supplemental licenses for the programs actually recorded.

11.6 Use of Copyright Office

The Copyright Office publishes a pamphlet entitled "How to Investigate the Copyright Status of a Work," Publication R22, which can be obtained free of charge from Information and Publications, Section LM-455, Copyright Office, Library of Congress, Washington, D.C. A copy of this pamphlet is attached to this Manual.

12. **Rights in Works Produced by Prince William County Public School Employees**

12.1 General

Works produced by Prince William County Public School employees are subject to the same rules and entitled to the same protection as any other work. This Section specifies the copyright holder, the means of obtaining copyright protection and the use of any royalties.

12.2 "Works Made for Hire"

Prince William County Public Schools shall be the copyright holder in all "works made for hire." Works made for hire include all works prepared by school employees within the scope of their duties, and any work ordered or commissioned from others, if specifically agreed by the parties.

12.3 Registering Prince William County Public Schools Copyrights

A. Materials intended for "one-time" use (including tests, answer sheets, course outlines and syllabi, and administrative memoranda) and forms shall not be registered.

B. Texts, articles, dramatic works, and works with intended artistic, literary or instructional merit will be forwarded to the Associate Superintendent for Instruction for a determination as to the need for registration.

12.4 Other Works Produced by Prince William County Public School Employees

Copyright to works produced by Prince William County Public School employees during non-working hours shall be held by the employee or such other person or entity as he or she may designate. Works produced during working hours shall be considered work-for-hire, whether or not such works are germane to the regular duties of the employee, unless prior permission of the superintendent or his designee to produce such works is obtained.

12.5 Variations in Copyright

Upon application, the Superintendent, in his or her sole discretion, may allow employees to retain some or all rights in a work, upon such terms and conditions as the Superintendent may deem appropriate.

12.6 Royalties

The superintendent shall determine license terms and conditions and the royalties, if any, to be charged for works owned by the Prince William County Public Schools. Royalties paid shall be disposed of in accordance with the financial and accounting regulations of the school system.

13. Student Works

13.1 General

Students produce a great many copyrightable works. The abuse of their rights in these works is a violation of both the Copyright Law and the system of ethics under which Prince William County Public Schools operate. Students shall be informed of their rights, and, where appropriate, assisted in protecting those rights.

13.2 Notice of Rights

In all classes in which creative effort is undertaken by students, the notice in Paragraph 13.3 shall be given to each student, or displayed in the classroom.

13.3 Rights in Student Works

You have the right to your own creative work. After the work has been reviewed, corrected, evaluated, or graded, the work will be returned to you. Except for classroom and instructional purposes, no one may publish, display, perform, record or transmit your work, or use your work as a part of another work without your permission. However, if you submit your work for publication, display or performance to any school activity, you are granting the school or school group the right to edit, publish, display, perform, record and transmit the work.

If you wish to register your work with the Copyright Office, write to Information and Publications, Section LM-455, Copyright Office,

Library ot Congress, Washington, D.C., and ask for publication RI, *Copyright Basics.*

13.4 Exceptional or Outstanding Works

Students who produce work of genuine merit, when judged against general artistic, literary, or other creative standards shall be so advised, and the instructor shall advise the student to consider registering his or her work with the Copyright Office.

13.5 School Publications

Works submitted to school publications or activities shall be used only for that publication or activity for which it has been submitted, unless the student's permission is obtained. School activities and publications which accept works for use shall have a right to record and transmit the work in addition to any other right. Copyright in the school publication or activity shall be held by the Prince William County Public Schools, but such works shall be registered only as provided in Paragraph 12.2(B).

13.6 Registration Fees

Students shall be responsible for completing all copyright registra-tion applications and paying the registration fees for their own works.

13.7 Responsibility of School

Nothing in this Section shall make Prince William County Public Schools liable for any damages or injury arising from failure to register a work, from infringement of any work by any person, whether or not a school employee, or from any other act or omission by any person not acting as an authorized agent of the Prince William County Public Schools.

APPENDIX I: COPYRIGHT POLICY EXAMPLES

COPYRIGHT POLICY #7

Instructional Council for Computers in Education (ICCE)
University of Oregon
1787 Agate Street
Eugene, Oregon 97403

Courtesy:

ICCE

ICCE Policy Statement on Network and Multiple Machine Software

Just as there has been shared responsibility in the development of this policy, so should there be shared responsibility for resolution of the problems inherent in providing and securing good educational software. Educators have a valid need for quality software and reasonable prices. Hardware developers and/or vendors also must share in the effort to enable educators to make maximum cost-effective use of that equipment. Software authors, developers and vendors are entitled to a fair return on their investment.

Educators' Responsibilities

Educators need to face the legal and ethical issues involved in copyright laws and publisher license agreements and must accept the responsibility for enforcing adherence to these laws and agreements. Budget constraints do not excuse illegal use of software.

Educators should be prepared to provide software developers or their agents with a district-level approved written policy statement including as a minimum:

1. A clear requirement that copyright laws and publisher license agreements be observed;
2. A statement making teachers who use school equipment responsible for taking all reasonable precautions to prevent copying or the use of unauthorized copies on school equipment;
3. An explanation of the steps taken to prevent unauthorized copying or the use of unauthorized copies on school equipment;
4. A designation of who is authorized to sign software license agreements for the school (or district);
5. A designation at the school site level of who is responsible for enforcing the terms of the district policy and terms of licensing agreements;
6. A statement indicating teacher responsibility for educating students about the legal, ethical and practical problems caused by illegal use of software.

Hardware Vendors' Responsibilities

Hardware vendors should assist educators in making maximum cost effective use of the hardware and help in enforcing software copyright laws and license agreements. They should as a minimum:

1. Make efforts to see that illegal copies of programs are not being distributed by their employees and agents;
2. Work cooperatively with interested software developers to provide an encryption process which avoids inflexibility but discourages theft.

Software Developers'/Vendors' Responsibilities

Software developers and their agents can share responsibility for helping educators observe copyright laws and publishers' license agreements by developing sales and pricing policies. Software developers and vendors should as a minimum:

1. Provide for all software a back-up copy to be used for archival purposes, to be included with every purchase;
2. Provide for on-approval purchases to allow schools to preview the software to ensure that it meets the needs and expectations of the educational institution. Additionally, software developers are encouraged to provide regional or area centers with software for demonstration purposes. The ICCE encourages educators to develop regional centers for this purpose;
3. Work in cooperation with hardware vendors to provide an encryption process which avoids inflexibility but discourages theft;
4. Provide for, and note in advertisements, multiple-copy pricing for school sites with several machines and recognize that multiple copies do not necessarily call for multiple documentation;
5. Provide for, and note in advertisements, network-compatible versions of software with pricing structures that recognize the extra costs of development to ensure compatibility and recognize the buyer's need for only a single copy of the software.

The Board of Directors of The International Council for Computers in Education approved this policy statement, with attachments, June 5, 1983.

The committee that drafted this policy included:

Jenny Better, Director of Curriculum, Cupertino Union Elementary District
LeRoy Finkel, San Mateo County Office of Education
Pennie Gallant, Apple Computer, Inc.
John Hazelwood/Jeffrey Armstrong, Corvus Systems, Inc.
Marion B. Kenworthy, Saratoga High School
Richard R. Monnard, Addison-Wesley Publishing Co.
Henry Vigil/Cliff Godwin, Cybertronics International
William Wagner, Santa Clara County Office of Education

ATTACHMENT 1
Suggested District Policy on Software Copyright

It is the intent of _____ to adhere to the provisions of copyright laws in the area of microcomputer programs. Though there continues to be controversy regarding interpretation of those copyright laws, the following procedures represent a sincere effort to operate legally. We recognize that computer software piracy is a major problem for the industry and that violations of computer copyright laws contribute to higher costs and greater efforts to prevent copies and/or lessen incentives for the development of good educational software. All of these results are detrimental to the development of effective educational uses of microcomputers. Therefore, in an effort to discourage violation of copyright laws and to prevent such illegal activities:

1. The ethical and practical problems caused by software piracy will be taught in all schools in the District.
2. District employees will be expected to adhere to the provisions of Public Law 96-517, Section 7(b) which amends Section 117 of Title 17 of the United States Code to allow for the making of a back-up copy of computer programs. This states that "...it is not an infringement for the owner of a copy of a computer program to make or authorize the making of another copy or adaptation of that computer program provided:
   a. that such a new copy or adaptation is created as an essential step in the utilization of the computer program in conjunction with a machine and that it is used in no other manner, or
   b. that such a new copy and adaptation is for archival purposes only and that all archival copies are destroyed in the event that continued possession of the computer program should cease to be rightful."
3. When software is to be used on a disk sharing system, efforts will be made to secure this software from copying.
4. Illegal copies of copyrighted programs may not be made or used on school equipment.
5. The legal or insurance protection of the District will not be extended to employees who violate copyright laws.
6. _____ of this school district is designated as the only individual who may sign license agreements for software for schools in the district. (Each school using the software also should have a signature on a copy of the software agreement for local control.)
7. The principal of each school site is responsible for establishing practices which will enforce this policy at the school level.

ATTACHMENT 2
Sample Software Policy of a Community College
with a Large Microcomputer Lab

It is the policy of this college that no person shall use or cause to be used in the college's microcomputer laboratories any software which does not fall into one of the following categories:

1. It is in the public domain.
2. It is covered by a licensing agreement with the software author, authors, vendor or developer, whichever is applicable.
3. It has been donated to the college and a written record of a bona fide contribution exists.
4. It has been purchased by the college and a record of a bona fide purchase exists.
5. It has been purchased by the user and a record of a bona fide purchase exists and can be produced by the user upon demand.
6. It is being reviewed or demonstrated by the users in order to reach a decision about possible future purchase or request for contribution or licensing.
7. It has been written or developed by _____ (college employee) for the specific purpose of being used in the _____ (college) microcomputer laboratory.

It is also the policy of the college that there be no copying of copyrighted or proprietary programs on computers belonging to the college

Source: De Anza College, Cupertino, California.

ATTACHMENT 3

Suggested Format of Software Licenses

1. Designated on a per site, district-wide or other geographic basis.
2. Requires the signature of a responsible school employee.
3. Includes provisions for a single copy purchase (with archival back-up copy) at full price.
4. Multiple-machine pricing:
   Includes provisions for a quantity discount for subsequent purchases of the same software provided:
   a. the purchase discount applies to a single purchase order.
   b. the purchase discount is noncumulative.
   c. the software is for the same computer type.
   i.e.: Radio Shack presently offers a 50% discount for purchases of 10 or more sets of the same software; Gregg/McGraw-Hill offers a discount schedule with incremental increases—buy 2, pay 10% less; 3—20% less; 4—30% less; 5 or more, 40% less.
5. Network pricing:
   May be offered as per school site or with quantity discount for school districts with multiple sites.
   Provide for a flat license fee for network-compatible versions of the software.
   ●flat fee provision is preferred over any variable rate based on number of computers or number of student users.
   ●network-compatibility, not just an unlocked version of the software, is required to eliminate the need for local reprogramming of copyrighted and licensed software.

   Include provision for purchase of multiple copies of documentation and accompanying materials.

   i.e.: A flat fee of two times the single copy retail price is offered to network users of Random House software.

APPENDIX II

TELEVISION SATELLITE INFORMATION

A. Communication Act of 1934, Title 47,
    UNITED STATES CODE, Section 605,
    Unauthorized Publication or
    Use of Communications

§ 605. Unauthorized publication or use of communications

Except as authorized by chapter 119, title 18, no person receiving, assisting in receiving, transmitting. or assisting in transmitting, any interstate or foreign communication by wire or radio shall divulge or publish the existence, contents, substance, purport, effect, or meaning thereof, except through authorized channels of transmission or reception, (1) to any person other than the addressee, his agent, or attorney, (2) to a person employed or authorized to forward such communication to its destination, (3) to proper accounting or distributing officers of the various communicating centers over which the communication may be passed, (4) to the master of a ship under whom he is serving, (5) in response to a subpoena issued by a court of competent jurisdiction, or (6) on demand of other lawful authority. No person not being authorized by the sender shall intercept any radio communication and divulge or publish the existence, contents, substance, purport, effect, or meaning of such intercepted communication to any person. No person not being entitled thereto shall receive or assist in receiving any interstate or foreign communication by radio and use such communication (or any information therein contained) for his own benefit or for the benefit of another not entitled thereto. No person having received any intercepted radio communication or having become acquainted with the contents, substance, purport, effect, or meaning of such communication (or any part thereof) knowing that such communication was intercepted, shall divulge or publish the existence, contents, substance, purport, effect, or meaning of such communication (or any part thereof) or use such communication (or any information therein contained) for his own benefit or for the benefit of another not entitled thereto. This section shall not apply to the receiving, divulging, publishing, or utilizing the contents of any radio communication which is transmitted by any station for the use of the general public, which relates to ships, aircraft, vehicles, or persons in distress, or which is transmitted by an amateur radio station operator or by a citizens band radio operator.

(June 19, 1934, ch. 652, title VI, § 605, 48 Stat. 1103; June 19, 1968, Pub. L. 90-351, title III, § 803, 82 Stat. 223; Sept. 13, 1982, Pub. L. 97-259, title I, § 126, 96 Stat. 1099.)

AMENDMENTS

1982—Pub. L. 97-259 struck out "broadcast or" after "communication which is", substituted "any station" for "amateurs or others", struck out "or" following "general public,", and substituted "ships, aircraft, vehicles, or persons in distress, or which is transmitted by an amateur radio station operator or by a citizens band radio operator" for "ships in distress".

1968—Pub. L. 90-351 inserted the introductory clause "Except as authorized by chapter 119, title 18", designated existing provisions as cls. (1) to (6), inserted "radio" preceding "communication" in second and fourth sentences, eliminated from third sentence "wire or" preceding "radio", and substituted "intercepted" for "obtained" in fourth sentence.

APPENDIX II: TELEVISION SATELLITE INFORMATION

B. Amendment to Communications Act, Public Law 98-549, October 1984, Section 705 (Replaces Section 605)

UNAUTHORIZED RECEPTION OF CERTAIN COMMUNICATIONS

Sec. 5. (a) Section 705 of the Communications Act of 1934 (as redesignated by section 6) is amended by inserting "(a)" after the section designation and by adding at the end thereof the following new subsections:

"(b) The provisions of subsection (a) shall not apply to the interception or receipt by any individual, or the assisting (including the manufacture or sale) of such interception or receipt, of any satellite cable programming for private viewing if—

"(1) the programming involved is not encrypted; and

"(2)(A) a marketing system is not established under which—

"(i) an agent or agents have been lawfully designated for the purpose of authorizing private viewing by individuals, and

"(ii) such authorization is available to the individual involved from the appropriate agent or agents; or

"(B) a marketing system described in subparagraph (A) is established and the individuals receiving such programming has obtained authorization for private viewing under that system.

"(c) For purposes of this section—

"(1) the term 'satellite cable programming' means video programming which is transmitted via satellite and which is primarily intended for the direct receipt by cable operators for their retransmission to cable subscribers;

"(2) the term 'agent', with respect to any person, includes an employee of such person;

"(3) the term 'encrypt', when used with respect to satellite cable programming, means to transmit such programming in a form whereby the aural and visual characteristics (or both) are modified or altered for the purpose of preventing the unauthorized receipt of such programming by persons without authorized equipment which is designed to eliminate the effects of such modification or alteration:

"(4) the term 'private viewing' means the viewing for private use in an individual's dwelling unit by means of equipment, owned or operated by such individual, capable of receiving satellite cable programming directly from a satellite; and

"(5) the term 'private financial gain' shall not include the gain resulting to any individual for the private use in such individual's dwelling unit of any programming for which the individual has not obtained authorization for that use.

"(d)(1) Any person who willfully violates subsection (a) shall be fined not more than $1,000 or imprisoned for not more than 6 months, or both.

"(2) Any person who violates subsection (a) willfully and for purposes of direct or indirect commercial advantage or private financial gain shall be fined not more than $25,000 or imprisoned for not more than 1 year, or both, for the first such conviction and shall be fined not more than $50,000 or imprisoned for not more than 2 years, or both, for any subsequent conviction.

"(3)(A) Any person aggrieved by any violation of subsection (a) may bring a civil action in a United States district court or in any other court of competent jurisdiction.

"(B) The court may-

"(i) grant temporary and final injunctions on such terms as it may deem reasonable to prevent or restrain violations of subsection (a):

"(ii) award damages as described in subparagraph (C); and

"(iii) direct the recovery of full costs, including awarding reasonable attorneys' fees to an aggrieved party who prevails.

"(C)(i) Damages awarded by any court under this section shall be computed, at the election of the aggrieved party, in accordance with either of the following subclauses;

"(I) the party aggrieved may recover the actual damages suffered by him as a result of the violation and any profits of the violator that are attributable to the violation which are not taken into account in computing the actual damages; in determining the violator's profits, the party aggrieved shall be required to prove only the violator's gross revenue, and the violator shall be required to prove his deductible expenses and the elements of profit attributable to factors other than the violation; or

"(II) the party aggrieved may recover an award of statutory damages for each violation involved in the action in a sum of not less than $250 or more than $10,000, as the court considers just.

"(ii) In any case in which the court finds that the violation was committed willfully and for purposes of direct or indirect commercial advantage or private financial gain, the court in its discretion may increase the award of damages, whether actual or statutory, by an amount of not more than $50,000.

"(iii) In any case where the court finds that the violator was not aware and had no reason to believe that his acts constituted a violation of this section, the court in its discretion may reduce the award of damages to a sum of not less than $100.

"(4) The importation, manufacture, sale, or distribution of equipment by any person with the intent of its use to assist in any activity prohibited by subsection (a) shall be subject to penalties and remedies under this subsection to the same extent and in the same manner as a person who has engaged in such prohibited activity.

"(5) The penalties under this subsection shall be in addition to those prescribed under any other provision of this title.

"(6) Nothing in this subsection shall prevent any State, or political subdivision thereof, from enacting or enforcing any laws with respect to the importation, sale, manufacture, or distribution of equipment by any person with the intent of its use to assist in the interception or receipt of radio communications prohibited by subsection (a).

"(e) Nothing in this section shall affect any right, obligation, or liability under title 17, United States Code, any rule, regulation, or order thereunder, or any other applicable Federal, State or local law".

(b) The amendments made by subsection (a) shall take effect on the effective date of this Act.

APPENDIX II: TELEVISION SATELLITE INFORMATION

C. Videotaping Off Satellite: A Consultant's Letter
    to a Client.

VIDEOTAPING OFF THE SATELLITE:
A CONSULTANT'S LETTER TO A CLIENT

The following is a copy of a letter from Jerome K. Miller, the president of Copyright Information Services, and a copyright consultant, to a client who requested a statement about the validity of a recent announcement by the Public Broadcasting System concerning videotaping educational programs transmitted via satellite. The letter has been edited to conceal the client's identity. A few additional changes were made to update the information. The letter is protected by U.S. copyright and is reproduced by permission of the author.

Dear :

As per your request, I evaluated the statement you sent me from the Public Broadcasting System (PBS). I have researched the communications law aspects of the PBS statement. The essence of the PBS statement appears in the second paragraph, which cites Title 47, *United States Code*, Sect 604, "Unauthorized publication or use of communications." This section gives the operators of every type of transmission system (telephone, microwave, radio, television, background music, etc.) comprehensive rights to prevent unauthorized persons and agencies from receiving, copying, transmitting, or otherwise using signals transmitted by their systems, including over-the-air transmissions. Limited exceptions are provided for law enforcement agencies, but no exceptions are provided for educators or others, unless the reception is authorized by the system operators. Congress recently amended the communications act to permit individuals to use satellite antennae to receive signals for their personal use in the home. That resolves a major issue over the use of satellite receivers by individuals, but a change affecting individual users does not provide any relief for educators who videotape programs directly from the satellite. In short, I think PBS and the individual program owners have you over a barrel and if they choose to file a complaint for illegal reception, transmission, or performance of their signals, you would have little basis for defense. The PBS statement also mentioned potential copyright infringements in videotaping from the satellites. The PBS statement does not cite a particular section of the copyright act, but Title 17, *U.S.C.*, Sect. 106 provides ample basis for a complaint of copyright infringement. The "Guidelines for Off-Air Recording of Broadcast Programming for Educational Purposes" (*Congressional Record*, Oct. 14, 1981, p. E4751) applies only to broadcast programming and does not appear to have direct application to copying from satellites, although the guidelines might be cited as stating the essence of videotaping as a form of fair use, regardless of the program source.

If a satellite operator sues an educational institution for videotaping from the satellite, he or she would appear to have a powerful basis for the action under Sect. 605 of the communications act and a reasonable basis under Sect. 106 of the copyright act. To put it in a nutshell, you appear to be vulnerable if you continue to copy off the satellite, unless you obtain clearance from the copyright proprietor and the transmitting agency.

A bill for this service is enclosed.

Sincerely

Jerome K. Miller
President

JKM/ws

APPENDIX II: TELEVISION SATELLITE INFORMATION

D. Addresses of French and Spanish
Language Satellite Programming

In discussing videotaping and performing video programs transmitted by satellite, many educators have expressed a desire to videotape French-language and Spanish-language programs off the satellite for use in foreign-language classes. The appropriate addresses for requesting licenses for these programs from two satellite sources are given here for your convenience.

Mr. Pierre Des Roches
Canadian Broadcasting Company
P.O. Box 6000
H3C3A8
Twelfth Floor
Montreal, Canada

French language transmissions on Anik D1, Transponders 15 and 16

Ms. Susan Catapano
Spanish International Network
250 Park Avenue
New York, NY 1001

Spanish language transmissions on Galaxy 1, Transponder 6

APPENDIX II: TELEVISION SATELLITE INFORMATION

E. Satellite Programming Directory

Reprinted by kind permission of:

The Home Satellite State of the Industry Report
February, 1986
CommTek Publishing Company
Boise, Idaho 83707

KEY SATELLITE PROGRAMMING

GALAXY 1

Tr. #	Service	Programming Category	Contact	Address	Affiliate Cost	Available To
2v	**TNN (The Nashville Network)** Country-oriented videos and programming. Discrete stereo on 5.58/5.76 MHz	Variety	Roy Mehlman (203) 965-6420 (203) 965-6000	Group W Satellite 41 Harbor Plaza Drive Stamford, CT 06904	Free	CATV
3h	**WGN — Chicago** Featuring movies, sports, specials, and syndicated programs.	Variety	Chris Bourne (918) 665-6690 (800) 331-4806	United Video Inc. 3801 S. Sheridan Road Tulsa OK 74145	10¢ sub/mo $100.00 min.	CATV,SMATV
4v	**The Disney Channel - East** Family entertainment, Matrix stereo on 5.8/6.8 MHz	Family	Vince Roberts (818) 840-7860 (800) 832-4636	4111 West Alameda Burbank, CA 91505	Varies	CATV
5h	**Showtime - East** First-run movies, sports and specials.	Movies and specials	Sales Dept. (212) 708-1600	1633 Broadway New York, NY 10019	Varies	CATV, SMATV, MDS, LPTV, DBS
6v	**SIN (Spanish International Network)** Spanish-language programming.	Ethnic	Susan Catapano (212) 502-1300	460 West 42nd St. New York, NY 10036	Pay affiliates for 24 hour coverage	CATV, LPTV, SMATV, broadcast
7h	**CNN (Cable News Network)** Live, round-the-clock news coverage and features	News	Marty Lafferty Patty Holland (SMATV) (404) 827-2250 (404) 827-2133	1050 Techwood Drive NW Atlanta, GA 30318	18¢ - 50¢ sub/mo/CATV Varies/SMATV	CATV, SMATV, LPTV, DBS, MDS, broadcast
8v	**CNN Headline News** Continuously updated 30-minute wheel of hard news.	News	Marty Lafferty Patty Holland (SMATV) (404) 827-2250 (404) 827-2133	1050 Techwood Drive NW Atlanta, GA 30318	Free/CATV Varies - 50¢/SMATV	CATV, SMATV, LPTV, DBS, MDS, broadcast
9h	**ESPN** Professional, college, and amateur sporting events.	Sports	Roger Williams (212) 661-6040	355 Lexington Avenue New York, NY 10017	19¢ sub/mo	CATV, SMATV

113

#	Service / Description	Category	Contact	Address	Price	Distribution
10v	**The Movie Channel - East** All-movie, commercial-free service. Matrix stereo on 5.8/6.8 MHz.	Movies	Sales Dept. (212) 708-1600	1633 Broadway New York, NY 10019	Varies	CATV, SMATV, LPTV, MDS
11h	**CBN Cable Network** Feature movies, classic comedy, westerns, children's programming and Christian inspirational (simulcast on F3, 8	Family	Tom Hohman (804) 424-7777	Virginia Beach, VA 23463	Free	CATV, SMATV
12v	**Reques TV(s)** First-run movies on a pay-per-view basis.	Movies	Richard Stone (212) 223-1073	150 E. 58 St. 39th Floor New York, NY 10155	Varies	CATV
13h	**C-SPAN** Daily, live coverage of the House of Representatives and House and Senate hearings	Public affairs	Brian Gruber (202) 737-3220	400 N. Capitol St. N.W. Washington, D.C. 20001	3¢/basic sub	CATV, LPTV, SMATV, MDS, DBS
14v	**The Movie Channel - West** All-movie, commercial-free service. Discrete stereo on 5.8/6.8 MHz	Movies	Sales Dept. (212) 708-1600	1633 Broadway New York, NY 10019	Varies	CATV, MDS, SMATV, LPTV
15h	**WOR - New York** Sports, movies and syndicated shows.	Variety	Gilbert Korta (315) 455-5955	Eastern Microwave P.O. Box 4872 Syracuse, NY 13221	10¢ sub/mo	CATV, SMATV
17h	**PTL - The Inspirational Network** Interdenominational family programming. Discrete stereo on 5.58/5.76 MHz (Simulcast F3.2)	Religious	Jack R. Hightower (704) 542-6000	PTL Center Charlotte, NC 28279	Free	CATV, SMATV, MDS, LPTV, DBS, broadcast
18v	**WTBS** Family-directed programming including sports, movies, syndication, and national and international news. Discrete stereo on 5.58/5.76 MHz	Family	Marty Lafferty Patty Holland (SMATV) (404) 827-2250 (404) 827-2133	SSS 8252 S. Harvard Tulsa, OK 74137	Varies	CATV, SMATV, MDS, DBS, broadcast
19h	**Cinemax - East (s)** First-run movies and specials.	Movies and specials	John Hagerty (212) 512-5440	HBO Building 1100 6th Ave. New York, NY 10036	Varies	CATV, SMATV
20v	**GalaVision** Spanish-language programming.	Ethnic	Andrew Goldman (212) 502-1300	460 West 42nd Street New York, NY 10036	Varies	CATV, SMATV, MDS

	Network	Type	Contact	Address	Cost	Distribution
21h	**USA Network - East** Sports-focused network also featuring special-interest programs	Variety	Gil Faccio (212) 408-9100	1230 6th Avenue New York, NY 10020	Basic 8.5¢ Tiered 14¢ - 25¢	CATV, SMATV
22v	**The Discovery Channel** Science, educational and variety programming.	Educational	Joe Maddox (301) 577-1999	Suite 1260 8201 Corporate Dr. Landover, MD 20785	Varies	CATV
22v	**AVN (Alternate View Network)** Educational and religious programming focusing on ethical and related issues.	Religious	Curtis A. Chambers (318) 226-8776	Head of Texas St. P.O. Drawer 1567 Shreveport, LA 71165	Free	CATV, SMATV, LPTV
23h	**HBO (Home Box Office) - East (s)** First-run movies, sports, and specials	Movies, specials, and sports	John Hagerty (212) 512-5440	HBO Building 1100 6th Ave. New York, NY 10036	Varies	CATV, SMATV
24v	**The Disney Channel - West** Family-oriented programming. Matrix stereo on 5.8/6.8 MHz	Family	Vince Roberts (818) 840-7860 (800) 832-4636	4111 West Alameda Burbank, CA 91505	Varies	CATV

GALAXY 1 AUXILIARY SERVICES

Tr. #	Service	Programming Category	Contact	Address	Affiliate Cost	Available To
3h	**Cable Sportstracker** Alphanumeric sports information service.	Sports	Chris Bourne (918) 665-6690 (800) 331-4806	United Video, Inc. 3801 S. Sheridan Road Tulsa, OK 74145	Varies	CATV,SMATV
3h	**The Electronic Program Guide** An hour-by-hour program guide in text format.	Unique	Chris Bourne (918) 665-6690 (800) 331-4806	United Video 3801 S. Sheridan Road Tulsa, OK 74145	$125/wk	CATV,SMATV
3h	**Moody Broadcasting Network** Variety religious programming.	Religious	Jim Goodrich (800) 621-7031 in IL (312) 329-4433	820 North LaSalle Chicago, IL 60610	Varies	CATV,SMATV, broadcast
3h	**Seeburg/Lifestyle Music** Monaural, commercial-free music intended for use with graphics channels, audio packages and FM Band	Music	Bonnie Sullivan (800) 334-1561 (919) 851-5823	Seeburg Music Library, Inc. 5706 New Chapel Hill Road Raleigh, NC 27607	1¢ sub/mo min. $40/mo max. $250/mo	CATV,SMATV, MDS, LPTV, DBS, STV, broadcast
3h	**StarShip Classical - WFMT** Fine arts and classical music transmitted in descrete stereo.	Music	Phyllis Vetters (918) 481-0881	SSS 8252 S. Harvard Tulsa, OK 74137	Varies	CATV, SMATV, MDS, broadcast
3h	**UPI Data Cable** 24-hour text news service in English and Spanish.	News	Jack Klinge (803) 771-6868	5970 S. Syracuse, Suite 157 Englewood, CO 80111	min. $185/mo	CATV, SMATV, MDS, LPTV
3h	**WFMT - Chicago** Fine arts/classical music.	Music	Chris Bourne (918) 665-6690 (800) 331-4806	United Video 3801 S. Sheridan Road Tulsa, OK 74145	2¢ per sub. FM hookups 20¢/sub	CATV, SMATV
13h	**All-Time Favorites** Adult contemporary format. One of nine channels in a package of premium music.	Music	Ann Stookey Stu Segal (703) 648-3200	StudioLine Cable Stereo 11490 Commerce Park Dr. Reston, VA 22091	$2.50/pay/sub/mo for all nine studioline services	CATV
13h	**Easy Listening** Easy listening format. One of nine channels in a package of premium music.	Music	Ann Stookey Stu Segal (703) 648-3200	StudioLine Cable Stereo 11490 Commerce Park Dr. Reston, VA 22091	$2.50/pay/sub/mo for all nine studioline services	CATV

13h	**The Classics** Classical format. One of nine channels in a package of premium music.	Music	Ann Stookey Stu Segal (703) 648-3200	StudioLine Cable Stereo 11490 Commerce Park Dr. Reston, VA 22091	$2.50/pay/sub/mo for all nine studioline services	CATV
13h	**Hit Country** Country and Western format. One of nine channels in a package of premium services.	Music	Ann Stookey Stu Segal (703) 648-3200	StudioLine Cable Stereo 11490 Commerce Park Dr. Reston, VA 22091	$2.50/pay/sub/mo for all nine studioline services	CATV
13h	**Super Hits** Top 40 format. One of nine channels in a package of premium services.	Music	Ann Stookey Stu Segal (703) 648-3200	StudioLine Cable Stereo 11490 Commerce Park Dr. Reston, VA 22091	$2.50/pay/sub/mo for all nine studioline services	CATV
15h	**The Greek Network** Music, news, sports, and specials in Greek.	Unique	Gilbert Korta (315) 455-5955	Eastern Microwave 112 Northern Concourse Box 4872, Syracuse, NY 13221	$8 sub/mo	CATV
15h	**The Italian Network** Music, news, sports, and specials in Italian.	Unique	Gilbert Korta (315) 455-5955	Eastern Microwave 112 Northern Concourse Box 4872, Syracuse, NY 13221	$8 sub/mo	CATV
15h	**WQXR - New York** Classical music broadcast in full discrete stereo.	Music	Gilbert Korta (315) 455-5955	Eastern Microwave 112 Northern Concourse Box 4872, Syracuse, NY 13221	$50/mo with WOR, $100 mo. without WOR	CATV
18v	**Dow Jones Cable News** Text service featuring stock tape and business news.	Unique	Dick Stickney (609) 452-2000	Box 300 Princeton, NJ 08540	0-15,000 - 1¢ 15-30,000 - ¾¢ Over 30,000 - ½¢	CATV, SMATV, LPTV, MDS, DBS
18v	**Keyfax National Teletext Magazine** Text service featuring news, sports, weather, and business.	News	Sales Dept. (918) 481-0881	SSS 3530 Bomar Rd. Douglasville, GA 30135	Varies	CATV, SMATV, MDS, broadcast
18v	**Electra Teletext Magazine** Text service featuring news, sports, weather, and business.	News	Sales Dept. (918) 481-0881	SSS 8252 South Harvard Tulsa, OK 74137	No programming charge; $4.95 decoder lease	CATV
18v	**SSS Cable Text** Color text featuring news, sports, weather, etc.	News	Sales Dept. (918) 481-0881	SSS 3530 Bomar Rd. Douglasville, GA 30135	Varies from $44.30 - $231.50/wk	CATV, SMATV, MDS, broadcast
18v	**AP News Cable** Text service featuring news, weather, sports, and business.	News, NYSE Tape	Greg Groce (202) 955-7213	1825 K Street NW Suite 615 Washington, D.C. 20006-1253	Varies from $46.50 weekly, max. $242.20 weekly	CATV, SMATV, LPTV, MDS, broadcast

Note: Special equipment is necessary to receive the avove VBI services.

SATCOM F3

Tr. #	Service	Programming Category	Contact	Address	Affiliate Cost	Available To
1v	**Nickelodeon - East** Designed for preschool through teen-age audiences.	Children	Mark Booth, Regional John Reardon, National (212) 484-8680	MTV Networks 75 Rockefeller Plaza New York, NY 10019	15¢ sub/mo	CATV
2h	**PTL - The Inspirational Network** Interdenominational family programming. Discrete stereo on 5.58/5.76 MHz. (Simulcast on G1, 17)	Religious	Jack R. Hightower (704) 542-6000	PTL Center Charlotte, NC 28279	Free	CATV, SMATV, MDS, LPTV, DBS, broadcast
3v	**TBN (Trinity Broadcasting Network)** Family Christian programming.	Religious	Stan Hollon (714) 832-2950	Trinity Broadcasting P.O. Box A Santa Ana, CA 92711	Free	CATV, MDS, LPTV, DBS, broadcast
4h	**FNN (Financial News Network)/SCORE** Live business and financial news. Sports news and occasional sporting events.	Sports and business news	Chris Taylor (213) 450-2412 (West) Peter Mondics (212) 888-7327 (East)	2525 Ocean Park Santa Monica, CA 90405	Varies	CATV, SMATV, DBS, MDS
5v	**Viewer's Choice(s)** First-run movies on a pay-per-view basis.	Movies	Sales Dept. (212) 708-1600	1633 Broadway Ave. New York, NY 10019	Varies	CATV
6h	**SPN (Satellite Program Network)** Movies, entertainment, how-to's, financial self-help programs, and video music.	Variety	Mark Dempsey (918) 481-0881	SSS 8252 S. Harvard Tulsa, OK 74137	Varies	CATV, SMATV, MDS, LPTV, DBS, broadcast
8h	**CBN Cable Network** Feature movies, classic comedy, westerns, children's pro-Family gramming, and Christian inspirational (simulcast on G1, 11).		Tom Hohman (804) 424-7777	Virginia Beach, VA 23463	Free	CATV, SMATV
9v	**USA Network - West** Sports-focused network also featuring special-interest programs.	Variety	Gil Faccio (212) 408-9100	1230 6th Avenue New York, NY 10020	Basic 8.5¢ Tiered 14¢ - 25¢	CATV, SMATV
10h	**Showtime - West** Commercial-free movies, sports, and specials.	Movies, sports, and specials	Sales Dept. (212) 708-1600	1633 Broadway New York, NY 10019	Varies	CATV, SMATV, MDS, LPTV

	Category	Contact	Address	Cost	Distribution
11v **MTV: Music Television** Advertiser-supported video music. Matrix stereo on 5.58/6.62 MHz. Digital stereo on 7.4 MHz.	Music	Mark Booth, Regional John Reardon, National (212) 484-8680	MTV Networks 75 Rockefeller Plaza New York, NY 10019	15¢ sub/mo	CATV
12h **EWTN (Eternal Word Television Network)** Catholic spiritual growth programming with family entertainment.	Religious	Ginger Scalici (205) 956-9537 (205) 956-3909 (E)	5817 Old Leads Road Birmingham, AL 35210	Free	CATV, SMATV
13v **HBO (Home Box Office) - West(s)** Movies, sports, and entertainment specials.	Movies, sports, and specials	John Hagerty (212) 512-5440	HBO Building 1100 6th Ave. New York, NY 10036	Varies	CATV, SMATV
15v **VH 1/Video Hits One** Advertiser-supported video music. Digital stereo on 5.8 MHz.	Music	Mark Booth, Regional John Reardon, National (212) 484-8680	MTV Networks 75 Rockefeller Plaza New York, NY 10019	15¢ sub/mo-Free with MTV-Varies without MTV	CATV
16h **HTN (Home Theater Network)** Family programming including movies (classics and comedy), specials, and travel. Multiplex stereo on 6.8 MHz.	Movies, specials, and travel	Kathy Peterson (207) 774-0300	465 Congress St. Portland, ME 04101	Varies	CATV, SMATV
16h **TLC (The Learning Channel)** Learning programs and college-credit courses for adults.	Educational	Lenda Washington (202) 331-8100	1200 New Hampshire Ave. #240 Washington, D.C. 20036	3¢ - 5¢ sub/mo	CATV, SMATV, MDS, LPTV
17v **Lifetime** Programming about health, relationships, self-development, and other self-help topics.	Lifestyles	Don Anderson (404) 952-4620 (203) 965-6576 (E)	Hearst/ABC-Viacom 1950 Spectrum Circle #B310 Marietta, GA 30067	Free	CATV
18h **Reuter Monitor Service(s)** News and price retrieval in commodity, money and investment markets.	News	Ron Owens (212) 732-2400	2 Wall Street New York, NY 10005	Varies	CATV, SMATV, MDS, LPTV, DBS, STV
18h **NJT (National Jewish Television)** Family Jewish programming	Religious	Joel Levitch (212) 549-4160	2621 Palisade Avenue Riverdale, NY 10463	Free	CATV, SMATV, DBS, LPTV, STV, broadcast
20h **BET (Black Entertainment Television)** Black-oriented movies, specials and sports. Mono/Audio at 6.2 and 6.8 MHz.	Ethnic	Carol Coody (202) 337-5260	1232 31st St. NW Washington, D.C. 20007	3¢ sub/mo	CATV, SMATV
21v **The Weather Channel** Live, constantly updated, national weather service.	Weather	Doug Holladay (404) 434-6800	2840 Mt. Wilkinson Pkwy. Atlanta, GA 30339	6¢ - 8¢ and 10¢ sub/mo	CATV

Tr.#	Service	Programming Category	Contact	Address	Affiliate Cost	Available To
22h	**HSN1 (Home Shopping Network 1)** Designed for shopping at home via television.	Unique	Charles Bohart (813) 530-0461	1529 US 19 South Clearwater, FL 33546	Free	CATV
22h	**USA Blackout Network** Programming that can be used in place of sports events that are blacked-out.	Unique	Andy Besch (212) 408-9100	1230 6th Avenue New York, NY 10020	Free (with primary feed)	CATV
23v	**Cinemax - West (s)** Commercial-free movies and specials.	Movies and specials	John Hagerty (212) 512-5440	HBO Building 1100 6th Ave. New York, NY 10036	Varies	CATV, SMATV
24h	**A&E (The Arts & Entertainment Network)** Distinctive entertainment from around the world. Discrete stereo on 5.58/5.76 MHz.	Entertainment	Andrew H. Orgel (212) 661-4500	Hearst/ABC-RCTV 555 Fifth Avenue New York, NY 10017	6¢ sub/mo	CATV

SATCOM F3 AUXILIARY SERVICES

Tr.#	Service	Programming Category	Contact	Address	Affiliate Cost	Available To
2h	**Satellite Radio Network** Gospel music, news, and ministries. (Simulcast on G1, 3 and F4, 17)	Religious	Mike Glinter (704) 552-2103	1 S. Executive Park, Ste. 403 Charlotte, NC 28287	Free	CATV, SMATV, broadcast
6h	**In Touch** Reading service for blind and physically handicapped. Volunteers read text from leading publications as well as daily newspapers.	Unique	Phyllis Vetters (918) 481-0881	SSS 8252 S. Harvard Tulsa, OK 74137	Varies	CATV, SMATV, MDS, broadcast
6h	**StarShip Hits** "Energy music to keep you moving." Upbeat sounds for dancing, exercising, and listening.	Music	Phyllis Vetters (918) 481-0881	SSS 8252 S. Harvard Tulsa, OK 74137	Free	CATV, SMATV, MDS, broadcast
6h	**StarShip Adult Contempory** Traditional MOR.	Music	Phyllis Vetters (918) 481-0881	SSS 8252 S. Harvard Tulsa, OK 74137	Varies	CATV, SMATV, MDS, broadcast

	Name / Description	Category	Contact	Address	Price	Distribution
6h	**StarShip Country And Western**	Music	Phyllis Vetters (918) 481-0881	SSS 8252 S. Harvard Tulsa, OK 74137	Varies	CATV, SMATV, MDS, broadcast
6h	**StarShip Comedy**	Music	Phyllis Vetters (918) 481-0881	SSS 8252 S. Harvard Tulsa, OK 74137	Varies	CATV, SMATV, MDS, broadcast
6h	**StarShip '50's, '60's, and 70's**	Music	Phyllis Vetters (918) 481-0881	SSS 8252 S. Harvard Tulsa, OK 74137	Varies	CATV, SMATV, MDS, broadcast
6h	**StarShip Big Bands**	Music	Phyllis Vetters (918) 481-0881	SSS 8252 S. Harvard Tulsa, OK 74137	Varies	CATV, SMATV, MDS, broadcast
7v	**ESPN Informational Network** Daily program schedules and advance event information.	Affiliate	Roger Williams (212) 661-6040	355 Lexington Avenue New York, NY 10017	19¢ sub/mo main service	CATV, SMATV
8h	**StarShip Jazz** Vocal and instrumental jazz, interviews, and discussions.	Music	Phyllis Vetters (918) 481-0881	SSS 8252 S. Harvard Tulsa, OK 74137	Varies	CATV, SMATV, MDS, broadcast
8h	**Genesis Cable Storytime** Children's storybooks in color computer graphics with silent text.	Children's	Arthur J. Doerksen (204) 949-1581	1036-167 Lombard Ave. Winnipeg, MB R3B OV3	Varies	CATV, SMATV
8h	**StarShip Contemporary Christian** Vocal and instrumental programs with spiritual vignettes.	Music	Phyllis Vetters (918) 481-0881	SSS 8252 S. Harvard Tulsa, OK 74137	Varies	CATV, SMATV, MDS, broadcast
8h	**StarShip Easy Listening**	Music	Phyllis Vetters (918) 481-0881	SSS 8252 S. Harvard Tulsa, OK 74137	Varies	CATV, SMATV, MDS, broadcast
16h	**Commodity Communications Corporation (s)** Quote service.	Unique	Bill Cassato (800) 621-2628 In IL: (312) 977-0990	420 Eisenhower Lane North Lombard, IL 60148	$90 - $585	CATV, Sat Net Cities

Tr. #	Service	Programming Category	Contact	Address	Affiliate Cost	Available To
19v	**Rhythm Mix** Urban contemporary/dance music. One of nine channels in a package of premium music.	Music	Ann Stookey Stu Segal (703) 648-3200	StudioLine Cable Stereo 11490 Commerce Park Dr. Reston, VA 22091	$2.50/pay/sub/mo for all nine studioline services	CATV
19v	**Album Tracks** Selections from hit albums. One of nine channels in a package of premium music.	Music	Ann Stookey Stu Segal (703) 648-3200	StudioLine Cable Stereo 11490 Commerce Park Dr. Reston, VA 22091	$2.50/pay/sub/mo for all nine studioline services	CATV
19v	**All That Jazz** Big bands and jazz format. One of nine channels in a package of premium music.	Music	Ann Stookey Stu Segal (703) 648-3200	StudioLine Cable Stereo 11490 Commerce Park Dr. Reston, VA 22091	$2.50/pay/sub/mo for all nine studioline services	CATV
19v	**StudioLine Specials** Specials and variety music. One of nine channels in a package of premium music.	Music	Ann Stookey Stu Segal (703) 648-3200	StudioLine Cable Stereo 11490 Commerce Park Dr. Reston, VA 22091	$2.50/pay/sub/mo for all nine studioline services	CATV

SATCOM F3 VBI AUXILIARY SERVICES

Tr. #	Service	Programming Category	Contact	Address	Affiliate Cost	Available To
6h	**Reuter News-View** Text service featuring general, financial, and sports news.	News	Kurt Hansen (212) 732-2400	2 Wall Street New York, NY 10005	3¢ - 5¢ sub/mo	CATV, SMATV STV, MDS, LPTV, DBS

Note: Special equipment is necessary to receive the above VBI services.

SATCOM F4

Tr. #	Service	Programming Category	Contact	Address	Affiliate Cost	Available To
1v	**HSN2 (Home Shopping Network 2)** Designed for shopping at home via television.	Unique	Charles Bohart (813) 530-0461	1529 US 19 South Clearwater, FL 33546	Free	CATV
2h	**Bravo** International films, award-winning film festivals, and performing arts. Multiplex stereo on 5.8/6.8 MHz.	Movies	Henry Gross (516) 364-2222	Rainbow Programming 100 Crossways Park West Woodbury, NY 11797	$1.95 sub/mo $3.00 sub/mo with AMC	CATV, SMATV, MDS
2h	**The C.O.M.B. Value Network** Designed for shopping at home via television.	Unique	Pat Minton (612) 539-8000	C.O.M.B. Co. 14605 28th Ave. N. Plymouth, MN 55441	Free	CATV, SMATV, MDS, LPTV, DBS, STV, broadcast.
4h	**Nickelodeon - West** Designed for preschool through teen-age audiences.	Children's	Mark Booth, Regional John Reardon, National (212) 484-8680	MTV Networks, Inc. 75 Rockefeller Plaza New York, NY 10019	15¢ sub/mo	CATV
6h	**BizNet, The American Business Network** Business and public affairs programming.	Business news	Frank Allen Philpot (202) 463-5817	U.S. Chamber of Commerce 1615 H Street NW Washington, D.C. 20062	Negotiable	CATV, LPTV, SMATV, broadcast
6h	**MSGN (Madison Square Garden Network)** Live sporting events from Madison Square Garden. Limited region.	Sports	Karen Metsky (212) 563-8980	4 Pennsylvania Plaza New York, NY 10001	None	CATV
7v	**NCN (National Christian Network)** Multi-denominational religious programs.	Religious	Ray Kassis (305) 632-1000	1150 West King Street Cocoa, FL 32922	Free	CATV, SMATV, MDS, LPTV, DBS, STV, broadcast
8h	**The People's Choice(s)** First-run movies on a pay-per-view basis.	Movies	Jerry Smith (203) 222-8930	274 Riverdale Ave. Westport, CT 06880	Varies	CATV, SMATV
9v	**SportsVision** Regional sports from the Chicago area.	Sports	Katie McEnroe (312) 296-0272	Rainbow Programming 1111 E. Touhy Ave, #280 Des Plaines, IL 60018	$4 - $4.50 sub/mo	CATV
10h	**AMC (American Movie Classics)** Movies made before 1970.	Movies	Henry Gross (516) 364-2222	Rainbow Programming 100 Crossways Park West Woodbury, NY 11791	$2.45 sub/mo $3.00 sub/mo with Bravo	CATV, SMATV, MDS

123

11v	**HSE (Home Sports Entertainment)** Regional sports from Texas, Louisiana, Arkansas, Oklahoma, and New Mexico.	Sports	Glen Gurgiolo (214) 988-9292	2080 N. SH360 Suite 260 Grand Prairie, TX 75050	Varies	CATV, broadcast
12h	**The Playboy Channel** Adult-oriented movies, comedy, and origninal programs.	Adult	Henry Gross (516) 364-2222	Rainbow Programming 100 Crossways Park West Woodbury, NY 11797	$3 - $3.55 sub/mo	CATV, SMATV, MDS
12h	**The Heartbeat Network** Family-oriented Christian programming.	Religious	Steve Rehburg (919) 376-6016	Total Christian Television P.O. Box 16 Burlington, NC 27216-0016	Free	CATV, SMATV, MDS, LPTV, DBS, STV, broadcast
13v	**NESN (New England Sports Network)** Regional sports service from New England.	Sports	John Claiburne (617) 536-9233	70 Brookline Ave. Boston, MA 02215	$3. - $5. sub/mo.	CATV, SMATV,
15v	**SNL (Success-N-Life)** **Educational, exercise, and variety.** **Christian programming.**	Religious	Tim Flynn (214) 620-7901	Word of Faith Outreach Center, Inc. P.O. Box 819000 Dallas, TX 75381	Varies	CATV
16h	**The Silent Network** Programming in sign language and voice.	Unique	Sheldon Altfeld (214) 654-6972	P.O. Box 1902 Beverly Hills, CA 90213	Free	CATV, LPTV
18h	**Hit Video USA** Contempory music videos.	Music	Mike Opelka (713) 650-0055	Woodlinger Broadcasting 35th Floor, Allied Bank Center Houston, TX 77002	Free	CATV, SMATV LPTV
19v	**WPIX - New York** Family-oriented programming, movies, and sports.	Variety	Chris Bourne (918) 665-6690 (800) 331-4806	United Video 3801 S. Sheridan Road Tulsa, OK 74145	10¢ sub/mo	CATV, SMATV
20h	**Prime Ticket** Regional sports coverage from the Los Angeles area.	Sports	Bob Steiner (213) 419-3274	Prime Ticket Los Angeles Forum Los Angeles, CA	Varies	CATV in specified areas
21v	**The Nostalgia Channel** Movies, comedy, and variety entertainment for all ages.	Family	Peter Flint (214) 869-0877	2 Dallas Communications Complex, Suite 225 Irving, TX 75039	$1.25 sub/mo	CATV, SMATV
22h	**HTS (Home Team Sports)** Sports from the Capital region.	Sports	Jim Bates (203) 965-6000	111 18th Street NV Suite 200 Washington, D.C. 20036	Varies	CAIV

23v	Odyssey Features, video, and a daily aerobics VJ targeted to the Music 18 - 49 age group. Discrete stereo on 5.58/5.76 MHz and monaural on 6.2 MHz.		Tom Shaw (305) 632-1000	1150 West King St. Cocoa, FL 32922	Free	CATV, SMATV, MDS, LPTV, DBS, STV, broadcast.
24h	Nightline Television Network Religious variety programming.	Religious	Mike Ward (803) 244-1616	P.O. Box 1616 Greenville, SC 29602	Free	CATV, SMATV, LPTV, MDS, DBS, STV

SATCOM F4 AUXILLIARY SERVICES

Tr. #	Auxiliary Service	Programming Category	Contact	Address	Affiliate Cost	Available To
7v	Family Radio Network (East) Noncommercial Bible-centered religious format with both music and talk programs.	Religious	Carl Gluck (712) 246-5151	Family Stations, Inc. 618 S. Sheridan Road Shenandoah, IA 51601	Free	CATV, broadcast
7v	Family Radio Network (West) Noncommercial Bible-centered religious format with both music and talk programs.	Religious	Carl Gluck (712) 246-5151	Family Stations, Inc. 618 S. Sheridan Road Shenandoah, IA 51601	Free	CATV, broadcast
17v	Satellite Jazz Network Stereo jazz service featuring contemporary and tradition jazz.	Music	Saul Levine (213) 475-8525	KKGO 10880 Wilshire Blvd., Ste. 2007 Los Angeles, CA 90024	Free	CATV, SMATV MDS, DBS, STV, broadcast
21v	National Broadcast Museum Superstation Vintage music and radio shows.	Music	Bill Bragg (214) 748-1112	National Broadcast Museum, Inc. 2001 Plymouth Rock Richardson, TX 75081	Free	CATV, SMATV, LPTV, MDS, DBS, STV broadcast.

TELESTAR 303

Tr. #	Service	Programming Category	Contact	Address	Affiliate Cost	Available To
1v	**CMTV (Country Music Television)** Country-oriented videos and programming. Discrete stereo on 5.58/5.76 MHz.	Music	Jim Cavazzini (212) 686-4340	30 East 40th Street, Ste. 507 Suite 507 New York, NY 10016	Free	CATV, SMATV, LPTV
2h	**Selec TV** Feature films and adult movies.	Movies, sports, and specials	Toni Cosenza (213) 827-4400 (213) 474-3500 (E)	4755 Alla Road Marina del Rey, CA 90291	$6.75 - $7.45 sub/mo	CATV, SMATV, MDS, LPTV, STV
18h	**American Extasy** Advertiser-supported X-rated movies.	X-rated Adult	Sales Department (212) 696-1221	419 Park Ave. S. Room 1400 New York, NY 10016	10¢ sub/mo	CATV, SMATV, DBS, LPTV MDS, STV
22h	**KTVT - Dallas** Featuring outdoor and specialty sports, movies, and syndicated programming.	Variety	Chris Bourne (916) 665-6690 (800) 331-4806	United Video 3801 Sheridan Road Tulsa, OK 74145	15¢ sub/mo	CATV, SMATV

WESTAR 5

Tr. #	Service	Programming Category	Contact	Address	Affiliate Cost	Available To
2v	**The University Network (The Unchannel)** Nonsecular programming with Dr. Gene Scott.	Unique	Larry Dudley (818) 246-8124	1501 South Glendale Avenue Glendale, CA 91205	20¢ sub/mo	CATV, SMATV, MDS, LPTV STV, broadcast
8v	**¡PASS (Pro Am Sports System)** Sports from Michigan, Ohio, and Indiana.	Sports	Bill Moren (313) 583-7600	500 Stephenson Highway Suite 204 Troy, MI 48083	Varies	CATV, STV
11h	**The Meadows Racing Network** Harness Racing	Sports	Marcy Hohn (412)339-7581	890 Constitution Blvd. New Kensington, PA 15068	Free	CATV, broadcast
24v	**The FUN Channel(s)** XXX-rated adult entertainment.	XXX-rated Adult	Space Age Video (408) 559-8812 (800) 221-9096	Space Age Video 2902 Almaden Exprwy. San Jose, CA 92125	$1.00 sub/mo encoded. Decoder required	CATV, SMATV DBS, LPTV MDS, STV
24v	**PPV - The Pay-Per-View Channel(s)** Adult movies and films and events on a pay per view basis.	Unique	Space Age Video (408) 559-8812 (800) 221-9096	Space Age Video 2902 Almaden Exprwy. San Jose, CA 92125	Varies	CATV, SMATV DBS, LPTV, MDS, STV, broadcast

WESTAR 5 AUXILIARY SERVICES

Tr. #	Service	Programming Category	Contact	Address	Affiliate Cost	Available To
2v	**Cable Radio Network** News, weather, sports, and music with cable highlights every 15 minutes.	Variety	Jim Roope (918) 352-7152	Cable Radio Network 10487 Sunland Blvd. Sunland, CA 91048	$100.00 sub/mo	CATV

127

SPACENET 1

Tr. #	Service	Programming Category	Contact	Address	Affiliate Cost	Available To
15h	**ACTS (American Christian Television System)** Family Christian entertainment.	Unique	Lloyd Hart (817) 737 3241	ACTS Satellite Network 6350 West Freeway Ft. Worth, TX 76150	Free	CATV,LPTV, SMATV

WESTAR 3 VBI AUXILIARY SERVICES

Tr. #	Service	Programming Category	Contact	Address	Affiliate Cost	Available To
1h	**AP News Cable** Occasional text transmission of general news and information.	AP	Greg Groce (202) 955-7213	1825 K Street NW Suite 615 Washington, D.C. 20006-1253	Varies	CATV, SMATV, MDS, LPTV
1h	**AP NewsPlus** Graphics-enhanced news.	AP	Greg Groce (202) 955-7213	1825 K Street NW Suite 615 Washington, D.C. 20006-1253	Varies	CATV, SMATV

Special equipment is necessary to receive the above VBI services.

v = vertical polarization   h = horizontal polarization
(Note c/i - commercial insertion, (E) - for after-hours transmission problems)
(s) = scrambled

APPENDIX II: TELEVISION SATELLITE INFORMATION

F. Article Providing Legal Discussion of
Reception of Programming from Satellites

Reprinted by kind permission of:

Willamette Law Review
Salem, Oregon 97301

THE COPYRIGHT ACT OF 1976 SERVED ON A SATELLITE DISH*

Willamette Law Review
21:1, Winter 1985

TABLE OF CONTENTS

---

*This paper was submitted as an entry in the Nathan Burkan Memorial Competition in Copyright Law.

COPYRIGHT POLICY DEVELOPMENT:
A RESOURCE BOOK FOR EDUCATORS

INTRODUCTION

In the last decade, technology has exploded into the American home. Home video recorders and satellite "dish" antennas are now not only household terms, but also increasingly common household fixtures. Communications satellites are positioned 22,300 miles above the equator where they remain stationary relative to the rotation of the earth.[1] Over one hundred space objects occupy this orbit, including at least ten commercial United States communication satellites.[2]

Satellite antennas intercept signals transmitted by these satellites and retransmit the signals to a receiver such as a television set or radio. Satellite dishes now cost less than $3,000 and can receive more than 140 television stations. The familiar looking dish-shaped antenna is now appearing in rural and suburban backyards across the United States. The age of the satellite dish has arrived.

Among the television signals which can be received by home satellite dishes are some which are meant to be received only by cable systems or broadcast stations.[3] Serious questions arise as to whether private viewer interception of pay cable signals is a violation of federal copyright law. The rapidly expanding use of satellite dishes makes it important to resolve the legal issues associated with them.[4]

This comment will consider whether a private home viewer violates federal copyright law by using a satellite dish to watch programs intended for pay cable subscribers.[5] Part I will discuss legal theories under which a copyright holder could potentially pursue a remedy for satellite dish interception of pay cable programming. Part II will evaluate the existing legal theories, and will suggest some possible legislative alternatives.

---

1. Perle, *Is the Bird Pie in the Sky? — Communication Satellites and the Law*, 27 BULL. COPYRIGHT SOC'Y U.S.A., 325, 325 (1980).

2. *Id. E.g.*, Comsat, Western Union's Westar and RCA's Satcom.

3. Piscitelli, *Home Satellite Viewing: A Free Ticket to the Movies?*, 35 FED. COM. L.J. 2 (1983).

4. Throughout its history, copyright law has not kept pace with evolving technology. Perhaps, as Justice Holmes said, "it is as it should be that the law is behind the times." O.W. HOLMES, COLLECTED PAPERS 294 (1920). In fact, copyright law began with the invention of the printing press. *Forward to* B. KAPLAN, AN UNHURRIED VIEW OF COPYRIGHT at vii-viii (1967).

The development and marketing of player pianos and perforated rolls of sheet music preceeded the Copyright Act of 1909. Sony Corp. of Am. v. Universal City Studios, 104 S. Ct. 774, 782-83 n. 11 (1984). *See* White-Smith Music Publishing Co. v. Apollo Co., 209 U.S. 1 (1908) (holding that player piano rolls did not violate the copyright on sheet music under the 1897 Act).

Section 198 of the Copyright Act of 1976, exempting library copying, is a Congressional response to innovation in copying techniques. *Sony*, 104 S. Ct. at 782-83 n. 11.

The technological capability to retransmit television signals by cable systems resulted in the compulsory licensing requirements embodied in Section 111 of the 1976 Act. *Id.*

The United States Supreme Court said, referring to home video recorders, "It may well be that Congress will take a fresh look at this new technology, just as it so often has examined other innovations in the past." *Id.* at 796.

5. Pay cable companies generally either own or lease the copyrights on programs they broadcast.

I. POTENTIAL SOURCES OF LIABILITY

A. Background

1. Satellite Television

Television broadcasters have used satellites since 1974 when CBS started to use Westar to transmit pay television.[6] Satellite broadcasts fit into four catagories: (1) donation supported and public service;[7] (2) superstation;[8] (3) advertiser supported;[9] and (4) subscriber supported.[10] Consumer use of satellite dishes has different effects on each kind of broadcaster.

For example, Fred Rogers, copyright owner of *Mr. Rogers' Neighborhood*, has testified that he had no objection to the home video recording of his television show because public programming is not royalty oriented.[11] Public broadcasters apparently share Fred Rogers' viewpoint that more widespread viewing of their programs is a service rather than a copyright infringement. Similarly, donation supported programmers are less concerned with copyright violations than are pay cable programmers.[12]

Superstations, on the other hand, are advertiser supported. The interception of signals by a home satellite dish should not result in a loss of revenue to the superstation. In fact, the superstation should receive an economic benefit from the increased advertising market.[13] The cable system operator carrying

---

6. *Communications Satellites: The Birds Are in Full Flight,* 19 BROADCASTING, Nov. 19, 1979, at 44.
Satellites have been used to broadcast live proceedings in the United States House of Representatives, sporting events, religious programming, and a full-credit course in "Communications Policy and the Law" given at NYU Law School and beamed to the McGeorge School of Law in Sacramento, California. Perle, *supra* note 1, at 327. Most recently, satellites enabled an entire criminal trial in New Bedford, Massachusetts, to be broadcast nationwide.
7. Public service television is supported by grants and donations. Examples of public service programming are *Sesame Street, Nova,* and *Masterpiece Theater.* The Christian Broadcasting Network is an example of donation supported broadcasting.
8. Superstations are simply local stations broadcast nationally via satellite. Atlanta's Channel 17 WTBS is an example of a "superstation." Ted Turner III formed Southern Satellite Systems, Inc. and leased a transponder on Satcom I. Channel 17's broadcast is aimed at the satellite and local cable systems throughout the United States are authorized to rebroadcast the signal to their viewers. Perle, *supra* note 1, at 329.
9. Entertainment Sports Programming Network (ESPN) is an example of advertiser supported cable. There is a small subscription fee, but ESPN depends on increased reception for larger advertising revenues.
10. Home Box Office, The Disney Channel, and Showtime are all subscriber supported broadcasts. Since there is no advertising, the subscription price is the sole source of revenue. This revenue, in turn, is used in part to pay copyright royalties.
11. *Sony,* 104 S. Ct. at 790 n. 27 *Mr Rogers' Neighborhood* is carried by more public television stations than any other program.
12. The Christian Broadcasting Network, for example, gives permission for home satellite dish owners to intercept its signals free of charge. *Small Earth Stations Blossom into Big Business,* BROADCASTING, Dec. 22, 1980, at 31, 34.
13. Piscitelli, *supra* note 3, at 3 n. 10. As noted in Perle, *supra* note 1, at 330 and n. 6, Turner claims a loss of advertising revenues to WTBS from satellite broadcasts. In a letter dated March 5, 1979, to J. Indelli, Divisional Sales Manager South of Metromedia Producers Corporation,

the superstation signal, however, does lose business to satellite dishes because the cable is no longer necessary to receive the signal.[14]

Like superstations, advertiser supported cable broadcasters realize more benefit than harm from satellite dishes.[15] A larger audience should result in a larger market for the advertisers that support the broadcast. Thus, higher advertising fees may be charged and the copyright holder should realize a higher royalty for the use of the work.

However, subscriber supported cable broadcasters, such as HBO, suffer from increased use of satellite dishes. Unlike the other three categories, pay cable depends on a restricted market. Unauthorized interception of pay cable signals dilutes the market of subscribers with possibly devastating results to the industry.[16] The most vocal objection to the unbridled use of home satellite dishes comes from pay cable operators.[17] The remainder of this article will focus on pay cable interception.

Turner explained:
> Let me outline some reasons for this dramatic loss of revenue.
> 1) *Federal Trade Commission (FTC) considerations:* There is a concern on the part of many advertisers that running commercials on WTCG-TV for products that are not available in all markets where our station is received by CATV homes is in violation of FTC regulations. For instance, the legal counsel for McCann-Erickson has advised their buyers not to run schedules on WTCG-TV for several major clients. Examples include A&P where the grocery prices differ from market to market, or even Coca-Cola where some packages are not universally available.
> Fast food advertisers, the #1 local television category, have cut back expenditures on our station because the majority of their spot commercials are for *local promotions* not available in all markets.
> Delta Airlines is buying other Atlanta stations but not WTCG-TV, because they use local destination commercial copy.
> 2) *Test Market Advertising:* This category represents a larger share of total spot dollars for most major advertisers than we had suspected. Procter and Gamble, for instance, has about half of its spot advertising dollars involved with various tests at any point in time. These advertisers shun WTCG-TV for these products because they cannot control the markets in which the commercials run.
> 3) *Talent Union Consideration:* The Screen Actors Guild (SAG) has put the advertisers and agencies on notice that they expect to be paid "wild spot" talent rates for every market in which the commercial is received by a cable system. In our situation this would mean that the cost of talent would exceed the cost of the commercial time by a factor as high as 100-to-1. Major agencies are not running on WTCG-TV because of this concern over the talent issue.
> We could give you additional examples of the above and a sheaf of specifics if you want.
> *But the net effect of this is that the additional cable households are costing WTCG-TV far more than they are benefiting the station.*

Id. *at 331 n. 6 (emphasis in original).*

14. *Id.* at 329.

15. Although ESPN broadcasts a claim that unauthorized viewing is "a violation of federal law," that conclusion is less than clear. *See* Cooper, *Install a Backyard Antenna to Tune in Satellite T.V.,* POPULAR SCI., March 1980, at 174.

16. Note, *Receive-Only Satellite Earth Stations and Piracy of the Airwaves,* 58 Notre Dame Law, 84, 85 (1982). *Cf.* National Subscription Television v. S & H TV, 644 F.2d 820, 826 (9th Cir. 1981) (economic effect of decoders on cable broadcasters).

17. *See Anti-Piracy Move: Scrambling HBO,* BROADCASTING, Feb. 22, 1982, at 58; *Small Earth Stations, supra* note 12, at 34.

Courts have not yet been asked to consider the legality of home satellite viewing. However, the Supreme Court did consider the application of copyright law to home video recording in *Sony Corp.* v. *Universal City Studios*.[18] Many of the arguments in that case, which will be discussed below, are applicable to the use of home satellite dishes. The basis of the *Sony* decision is the Copyright Act of 1976.[19] Thus, the 1976 Act is the appropriate starting point to determine whether home use of satellite dishes infringes upon legal rights of pay cable programmers.

2. The Copyright Act of 1976

In 1976, Congress enacted the first comprehensive revision of the Copyright Act of 1909. While recodifying the principles of the 1909 Act,[20] the new act benefits from a considerable body of case law.

Several provisions of the 1976 Act differ substantially from the 1909 Act. The 1976 Act extended federal copyright protection to any original work "fixed in any tangible medium of expression."[21] Another change is in the

---

18. 104 S. Ct. 774 (1984).

19. Copyright Act of 1976, 17 U.S.C. §§ 101-810 (1982).

20. Regarding copyrightable works, compare Copyright Act of 1909, ch. 320 § 5, 35 STAT. 1075, 1076, with 1976 Act, 17 U.S.C. § 102(a). The original works of authorship include (in addition to television):
(1) literary works;
(2) musical works, including any accompanying words;
(3) dramatic works, including any accompanying music;
(4) pantomimes and choreographic works;
(5) pictorial, graphic, and sculptural works;
(6) motion pictures and other audiovisual works; and
(7) sound recordings.
17 U.S.C. § 102(a).
Regarding exclusive rights protected, compare 1909 Act, ch. 320 § 1, 35 STAT. 1075, with 1976 Act, 17 U.S.C. § 16. The exclusive rights protected now are:
(1) to reproduce the copyrighted work in copies or phonorecords;
(2) to prepare derivative works based upon the copyrighted work;
(3) to distribute copies or phonorecords of the copyrighted work to the public by sale or other transfer of ownership, or by rental, lease, or lending;
(4) in the case of literary, musical, dramatic, and choreographic works, pantomimes, and motion pictures and other audiovisual works, to perform the copyrighted work publicly, and
(5) in the case of literary, musical, dramatic, and choreographic works, pantomimes, and pictorial, graphic, or sculptural works, including the individual images of a motion picture or other audiovisual work, to display the copyrighted work publicly.
17 U.S.C. § 106.
Regarding remedies for infringement of a copyright, compare 1909 Act. ch. 320 § 25, 35 STAT. 1075, 1081, *amended by* Act of August 24, 1912, ch. 356, 37 STAT. 488, 489, with 1976 Act. 17 U.S.C. § 501-09. Remedies include actual damages, statutory damages, and attorneys' fees.

21. 17 U.S.C. § 102(a). However, the legislative history indicates that live broadcasts are *not* "fixed" and therefore not included within the Act. *See* H.R. REP. No. 1476, 94th Cong., 2d Sess. 1, 52-53 (1976), *reprinted in* 1976 U.S. CODE CONG. & AD. NEWS 5659, 5666. The Act provides that works not fixed in a tangible medium of expression may be protected by other rights, common law, or state statutes. 17 U.S.C. § 301(b).

length of time copyright protection is provided. The new Act allows a single period of protection, usually extending 50 years beyond the death of the author,[22] rather than the original renewable 28-year period.[23]

In 1909 Congress did not anticipate the development of television. The definition of "publication" in the 1909 Act was not broad enough to include television reception.[24] Thus, producers of television programs were often forced to resort to common law protection for their work. The 1976 Act filled that gap by providing protection from the date of "fixation,"[25] thereby eliminating the need to rely on state law doctrines. The 1976 Act anticipates technological advances by providing that fixation can occur in any tangible medium "now known or later developed" from which the work can be "communicated, either directly or with the aid of a machine."[26] Specifically, protection is provided for "motion pictures and other audiovisual works."[27]

If protection is provided to television under the Act, the copyright holder has the following enumerated rights:
(1) to reproduce the copyrighted work in copies or phonorecords;
(2) to prepare derivative works based upon the copyrighted work;
(3) to distribute copies or phonorecords of the copyrighted work to the public by sale or other transfer of ownership, or by rental, lease, or lending;
(4) ... to perform the copyrighted work publicly;

---

22. 17 U.S.C. § 302. Special provisions cover works created prior to 1978, anonymous works, and works made for hire. *See 17 U.S.C.* §§ 302-04.

23. 1909 Act, ch. 320, § 23, 35 STAT. 1075, 1080.

24. *See* King v. Mister Maestro, Inc. 224 F. Supp. 101 (S.D.N.Y. 1963) (live broadcast of "oral delivery" of speech on radio and television not a publication of written text of speech).

25. 17 U.S.C. § 102(a). A work is "fixed" when its embodiment in a copy or phonorecord...is sufficiently permanent or stable to permit it to be perceived, reproduced, or otherwise communicated for a period of more than transitory duration." 17 U.S.C. §101:

26. 17 U.S.C. § 102(a).

27. 17 U.S.C. § 102(a)(6). *See supra* note 20. Definitions of terms used in § 102(a)(6) are provided by § 101:

> "Audiovisual works" are works that consist of a series of related images which are intrinsically intended to be shown by the use of machines, or devices such as projectors, viewers, or electronic equipment, together with accompanying sounds, if any, regardless of the nature of the material objects, such as films or tapes, in which the works are embodied."
>
> "Motion pictures" are audiovisual works consisting of a series of related images which, when shown in succession, impart an impression of motion, together with accompanying sounds if any." 17 U.S.C. § 101.
>
> Most commercial television programs, if fixed on film or tape at the time of broadcast or before, qualify as "audiovisual works." Since the categories set forth in § 102(a) are not mutually exclusive, a particular television program may also qualify for protection as a dramatic, musical, or other type of work.

Sony, 104 S. Ct. at 798-99 n.5 (Blackmun, J., dissenting).

A technical "legitimate view" of the technology involved reveals that television, unlike a motion picture, is not a series of individual pictures. A television picture is a series of dots arranged in lines on the screen which results in an ever changing flow of images. Piscitelli, *supra* note 3, at 6.

(5)... to display the copyrighted work publicly.[28]
Home satellite viewing potentially infringes upon the rights of reproduction, public performance, and public display.

B. *Potential Copyright Actions*

To maintain a cause of action for use of a satellite dish in violation of the 1976 Act, a copyright holder must show either 1) that the satellite dish owner must obtain the compulsory license required by Section 111 of the 1976 Act, or 2) that an enumerated copyright has been violated. The copyright holder must also show that the use of the work in question was "unfair" under Section 107 of the 1976 Act.[29]

1. *Section 111 of the Copyright Act of 1976*

Section 111 of the 1976 Act[30] may resolve whether interception of pay television signals by a satellite dish is a copyright infringement. Section 111 is a Congressional response to Supreme Court decisions holding that there was no violation of federal copyright law when cable companies rebroadcast television programs.[31]

In *Fortnightly Corp. v. United Artists Television*, the Court held that cable system operators did not violate the Copyright Act by intercepting television signals and wiring those signals to subscribers.[32] In *Fortnightly*, the cable company provided a television signal to viewers in a mountainous region of West Virginia where a conventional antenna would not receive the broadcast. The Court stated: "One who manually or by human agency merely actuates electrical instrumentalities, whereby inaudible elements that are omnipresent in the air are made audible to persons who are within hearing, does not perform within the meaning of the Act."[33]

In a similar case, *Teleprompter Corp. v. Columbia Broadcasting System*,[34] the television signal was extended to an area where it had not previously been received. The Court reiterated its holding that cable transmission was essentially a viewing function "irrespective of the distance between

---

28. 17 U.S.C. § 106. Copyrights are different from patents in that copyrights do not confer an absolute monopoly upon the owner. A copyright owner's rights are only those enumerated in the statute. Unless one of those enumerated rights is violated, unlimited use of a copyrighted work will not constitute an infringement. *See* Piscatelli, *supra* note 3, at 4. *See generally, Sony*, 104 S. Ct. 774 (home video recording of copyrighted material not an infringement); Teleprompter Corp. v. Columbia Broadcasting System, 415 U.S. 394 (1974) (cable companies did not violate any rights of copyright owners by retransmission of broadcasts).
29. *See infra* notes 68-97 and accompanying text.
30. 17 U.S.C. 111.
31. The legislative history of § 110 suggests that section 111 was a legislative compromise worked out between copyright owners, broadcasters, and cable system operators. H.R. REP. No. 1476, 94th Cong., 2d Sess. 88-91, *reprinted in* 1976 U.S. CODE CONG. & AD. NEWS at 5703-05.
32. 392 U.S. at 402.
33. *Id.* at 398 n.24 (*quoting* Buck v. Debaum, 40 F.2d 734, 735 (1929)).
34. 415 U.S. 394, (1974).

the broadcasting station and the ultimate viewer."[35] Satellite viewing is the next logical step — remove the wires and reach even more remote areas. The reasoning of the Court in *Fortnightly and Teleprompter*, however, is unlikely to be extended to satellite dishes.

Section 111 of the 1976 Act requires a compulsory license for cable system operators to make secondary transmissions[36] of broadcasts including copyrighted works.[37] In the 1976 Act, Congress established three classifications of secondary transmissions: (1) those completely exempt from § 111 liability,[38] (2) those requiring compulsory licensing,[39] and (3) those afforded full copy-

---

35. *Id.* at 408.

36. A "secondary transmission" is the further transmitting of a primary transmission simultaneously with the primary transmission, or nonsimultaneously with the primary transmission by a "cable system" not located in whole or in part within the boundary of the forty-eight contiguous states, Hawaii, or Puerto Rico....
17 U.S.C. § 111(f).

37. 17 U.S.C. § 111(d). Broadcasters pay a copyright fee to the Copyright Royalty Tribunal to obtain the license. Secondary transmissions can then be simultaneous with the broadcast if the programming and advertising content is not altered by the cable system. *See* Perle, *supra* note 3, at 332.

38. Basically these are secondary transmissions: (1) to hotel guests, (2) for educational purposes, (3) where the cable system operator does not control the signal's content, and (4) by nonprofit organizations or govermental agencies. The Act imposes technical limitations that warrant close examination:
(a) Certain Secondary Transmissions Exempted — The secondary transmission of a primary transmission embodying a performance or display of a work is not an infringement of copyright if —
(1) the secondary transmission is not made by a cable system, and consists entirely of the relaying, by the management of a hotel, apartment house or similar establishment, of signals transmitted by a broadcast station licensed by the Federal Communications Commission, within the local service area of such station, to the private lodgings of guests or residents of such establishment, and no direct charge is made to see or hear the secondary transmission; or
(2) the secondary transmission is made soley for the purpose and under the conditions specified by clause (2) of section 110; or
(3) the secondary transmission is made by any carrier who has no direct or indirect control over the content or selection of the primary transmission or over the particular recipients of the secondary transmission, and whose activities with respect to the secondary transmission consist solely of providing wires, cables, or other communications channels for the use of others; *Provided,* That [sic] the provisions of this clause extend only to the activities of said carrier with respect to secondary transmissions and do not exempt from liability the activities of others with respect to their own primary or secondary transmissions; or
(4) the secondary transmission is not made by a cable system but is made by a govermental body, or other non-profit organization, without any purpose of direct or indirect commercial advantage, and without charge to the recipients of the secondary transmission other than assessments necessary to defray the actual and reasonable costs of maintaining and operating the secondary transmission service
17 U.S.C. § 111(a).

39. A cable system operator, under this classification, may retransmit any work allowed by the Act so long as he makes periodic accountings and payments to the copyright office. 17 U.S.C. § 111(c)-(d). The fee is determined by the revenue received by the cable system operator from subscribers. § 111(d)(2). Under the terms of the Act, the operator may not alter any signal that it retransmits. § 111(c)(3). Fees are paid to the copyright office and distributed to copyright owners through the Copyright Royalty Tribunal. § 111(d)(3), (4).

right protection.[40] Section 111 makes it clear that a retransmission of another cable system's signal containing copyrighted works,[41] as well as the retransmission of a pay television signal,[42] is a copyright infringement. Whether or not § 111 is controlling depends on the breadth the courts attach to the compulsory licensing provisions.

"Cable systems" are authorized to recieve the compulsory license under § 111(c). As defined by the Act, a "cable system" is one that:

> receives signals transmitted or programs broadcast by one or more television broadcast stations ... and makes secondary transmissions of such signals or programs by wires, cables, *or other communications channels to subscribing members of the public who pay for such service* ....[43]

This definition is broad enough to include a satellite broadcast signal received by domestic satellite dishes.[44] If a satellite broadcaster is included as a cable system operator, then it would be subject to § 111. On the other hand, a home viewer does not come within the definition of cable system operator because he has nothing to do with transmitting the satellite signal. Therefore, § 111 does not answer the question of whether his use of a satellite dish is a copyright violation.[45]

---

40. Pay television is included among those afforded full copyright protection. Section 111(b) reads:

> (b) Secondary Transmission of primary transmission to controlled group —
> Notwithstanding the provisions of subsections (a) and (c), the secondary transmission to the public of a primary transmission embodying a performance or display of a work is actionable as an act of infringement under section 501 ... if the primary transmission is not made for reception by the public at large but is controlled and limited to reception by particular members of the public.

17 U.S.C. § 111(b).

41. 17 U.S.C.§ 110(a).

42. "[T]he second transmission . . . is actionable as an act of infringement . . . if the first transmission . . . is controlled and limited to reception by particular members of the public . . ." 17 U.S.C. § 111(b).

43. 17 U.S.C. § 111(f) (emphasis added).

44. Samuels, *Copyright and the New Communications Technologies*, 25 N.Y.L. SCH. L. REV. 905, 912 (1980).

45. Section 110 of the 1976 Act exempts from the compulsory license system public reception "on a single receiving apparatus of a kind commonly used in private homes" for which no direct charge is made and which is not further transmitted to the public. 17 U.S.C. § 110(5). In section 110, Congress codified the judicial decisions regarding the use of television and radio signals by hotels and restaurants. *See, e.g.*, Twentieth Century Music Corp. v. Aiken, 422 U.S. 151, 155 (1975) (no infringement where a radio signal was played over four speakers in a fast-food restaurant).

Section 110's application to home satellite dishes, however, would be misplaced, because the exemption refers only to public and not to private viewing. More importantly, the exemption does not anticipate intercepted signals of the kind a satellite dish is capable of receiving. Therefore, the exemption is probably inapplicable to a case where a satellite dish is intercepting a pay television signal.

2. The Right of Reproduction

The 1976 Act gives the copyright holder the right to forbid the reproduction of the work in copies or phonorecords.[46] "Copies" are material objects in which a work is fixed.[47] A "fixed work," as defined by the 1976 Act, is one that "is sufficiently permanent or stable to permit it to be perceived, reproduced, or otherwise communicated for a period of more than transitory duration."[48] As noted in *Sony*,[49] a television broadcast transmitted by satellite is probably fixed for the purposes of the Act. A copy of the broadcast would violate the right of reproduction, at least if the broadcast was an audiovisual work.[50] [51]

Virtually all television programs qualify as audio visual works because they are prerecorded or taped at the time of broadcast. But is the unauthorized interception and display of a television broadcast a reproduction? Probably not. The legislative history of the 1976 Act indicates that the right of display, but not the right of reproduction, may be violated by unauthorized interception and display of a broadcast. Thus, an action claiming that the use of a satellite dish violates the right of reproduction would probably fail.

3. The Right of Public Performance

The copyright holder has the exclusive right to permit public performances of his work.[52] To "perform" a motion picture is to show its images in any sequence or to make its soundtrack audible.[53] Similarly, a broadcast of a taped television program is a performance of the program. To constitute an infringement, however, the performance must be public:

Tc perform or display a work "publicly" means—
(1) to perform or display it at a place open to the public or at any place where a substantial number of persons outside of a normal circle of a

---

46. 17 U.S.C. § 106(1).

47. 17 U.S.C. § 101. *See supra* note 25 and accompanying text.

48. 17 U.S.C. § 101.

49. 104 S. Ct. at 798 n.3 (Blackmun, J. dissenting).

50. In his *Sony* dissent, Justice Blackmun said: "[M]ost television programs, *if fixed on film or tape at the time of broadcast or before*, qualify as 'audiovisual works.'" 104 S. Ct. at 798 n.5 (emphasis added).

Justice Blackmun suggests that a particular television program may qualify as a dramatic, musical, or other type of work. *Id.* Justice Blackmun's analysis is similar to that referred to by Piscatelli, *supra* note 3, at 5, as a "strict tangibleness" standard.

51.   "Reproduction" under clause (1) of section 106 is to be distinguished from "display" under clause (5). For a work to be "reproduced," its fixation in tangible form must be "sufficiently permanent or stable to permit it to be perceived, reproduced or otherwise communicated for a period of more than transitory duration." Thus, the showing of images on a screen or tube would not be a violation of clause (1), although it might come within the scope of clause (5).

S. REP. No. 473, 94th Cong., 1st Sess. 58 (1976).

52. 17 U.S.C. § 106(4).

53. 17 U.S.C. § 101.

family and its social acquaintances is gathered; or

(2) to transmit or otherwise communicate a performance or display of the work to a place specified by clause (1), or to the public, by means of any device or process, whether the members of the public capable of receiving the performance or display receive it in the same place or in separate places and at the same time or at different times.[54]

Home viewers do not seem to be participating in a public performance under clause (1). However, under clause (2), because satellite dishes communicate the broadcast to an unintended scattered audience, there may be a public performance.[55] If there is a public performance, rights of copyright holders, such as broadcasting companies who either own or lease a valid copyright on their programming, may be infringed.

At first glance, case law suggests that reception of satellite signals would not be a public performance. The Supreme Court ruled, under the 1909 Act, that "Broadcasters perform. Viewers do not perform."[56]

The question of public performance was not addressed by the majority in *Sony*. The dissent, however, applied the evident intent of the 1976 Act: "Like 'sing[ing] a copyrighted lyric in the shower,'... watching television at home with one's family and friends is now considered a performance."[57] Therefore, home viewing of television programs intercepted by a satellite dish probably would be considered a performance under the 1976 Act.

Section 106(4) of the 1976 Act only prohibits unauthorized *public* performance. Justice Blackmun, in his dissent, further asserted that "[h]ome television viewing...does not infringe any copyright...because § 106(4) contains the [word] 'publicly'."[58] However, his analysis will probably not apply to satellite dishes for two reasons. First, the opinion was not concerned with intercepted signals not intended for use by the general public, such as a pay television signal.

---

54. *Id. See generally*, 2 M. NIMMER, NIMMER ON COPYRIGHT § 8.01 (1984).

55. The "scatter-audience concept conceivable could lead to the conclusion that several hundred individual viewers, each 'performing' by turning on their satellite receivers," amounts to a public performance. Piscitelli, *supra* note 3, at 7. Such a result is particularly possible under the 1976 Act since the "for profit" requirement of the 1909 Act has been eliminated. *Id.* at 7 n.38.

56. Fortnightly Corp. v. United Artists Television, 392 U.S. 390, 398 (1968) (citations omitted).

57. 104 S. Ct. at 802 (Blackmun, J. dissenting) (*quoting* Twentieth Century Music Corp. v. Aiken, 422 U.S. 151, 155 (1975)). Justice Blackmun further explained:

> In a trio of cases, *Fortnightly Corp. v. United Artists, Teleprompter Corp. v. Columbia Broadcasting System, Inc.,* and *Twentieth Century Music Corp. v. Aiken,* this Court held that the reception of a radio or television broadcast was not a "performance" under the 1909 Act. The Court's "narrow construction" of the word 'perform' was "completely overturned by the [1976 Act] and its broad definition of "perform" in section 101." 1976 House Report 87, U.S. CODE CONG. & ADMIN. NEWS 1976, p. 5701.

104 S. Ct. at 802 n. 17 (citations omitted). This is a dissent, but because it was a 5-4 decision and the dissent is well written, it is plausible that on the facts of a satellite dish case this reasoning could be persuasive.

58. 104 S. Ct. at 802.

Second, and more importantly, the dissent did not consider the scattered-audience definition of public performance under the 1976 Act.[59] The Act's definition of "publicly" includes the communication of a work to people in different places at different times. The effect of home satellite dishes intercepting a pay television signal is the same as a broadcaster's illicit transmission of a copyrighted program.

At best, the 1976 Act is ambiguous as to whether home viewing of satellite signals constitutes a public performance. By amending the 1976 Act, Congress could clarify whether the use of home satellite dishes constitutes a public performance. Short of that, the copyright Act itself may provide other avenues of protection for the copyright holder.

4. The Right of Public Display

The 1976 Act codified the right of a creator to control the public display of his work.[60] Although some commentators believe that the display right is limited to the electronic transmission of a printed version of a work,[61] others suggest that the display right is better suited for copyright protection from satellite dish interception.[62] There are several reasons why the display right may be the best basis for copyright protection under the existing law.

Unlike the right of reproduction, the right of display is not subject to a "strict tangibleness" interpretation.[63] Additionally, there is no broadcaster/-viewer distinction as there is under the right of public performance.[64] Although the public/private dichotomy must still be overcome, the scattered-audience definition of "public" is equally applicable to public display as to public performance.[65]

Congress has indicated that the scattered-audience definition of "publicly" is intended for "public display":

> [P]ublic display include[s]...acts that transmit or otherwise communicate a performance or display of the work to the public by means of any device or process. The definition of "transmit"...is broad enough to include all conceivable forms and combinations of wired or wireless communications media, including but by no means

---

59. *See supra* note 55 and accompanying text.
60. 17 U.S.C. 106(5). "Clause (5) of Section 106 represents the first explicit statutory recognition in American copyright law of an exclusive right to show a copyrighted work, or an image of it, to the public." S. REP. 473, 94th Cong., 1st Sess., 58 (1976).
61. NIMMER, *supra* note 54, at § 8.20(A).
62. Piscitelli, *supra* note 3, at 9. The statute specifies "television image" as a means of display and the legislative history discusses "the showing of images on a screen." *Id.* at 11 n.58.
63. 17 U.S.C. § 101.
64. *See supra* notes 54-57 and accompanying text.
65. No court has yet considered this issue. *See supra* note 55 and accompanying text.

limited to radio and television broadcasting as we know them.[66]

A scattered audience could be publicly displaying a program by the "showing of an image on a cathode ray tube..."[67] Therefore, the public display right possible makes satellite dish interception of pay television signals a copyright infringement.

5. *The Fair Use Doctrine's Limitation on Copyright Infringement*

So far, this section has discussed applications of the statutory rights of a copyright holder provided by the 1976 Act. The federal copyright laws have never granted a copyright holder complete control over his work.[68] "Any individual may reproduce a copyrighted work for a 'fair use'; the copyright owner does not possess the exclusive right to such a use."[69]

As one of the most progressive changes in the 1976 Act, Congress codified the doctrine of fair use.[70] Courts have traditionally considered certain uses and reproductions of copyrighted works "fair uses" and therefore non-infringing.[71] The legislative history of § 107 shows that Congress intended it "to restate the present judicial doctrine of fair use, not to change, narrow, or enlarge it in any way."[72]

Sony Corp. v. Universal City Studios is the first major case to consider the

---

66. H.R. REP. No. 1476, 94th Cong., 2d Sess. 64, *reprinted in* 1976 U.S. CODE CONG. & AD. NEWS 5659, 5678.

67. *Id.* at 5677.

68. *See, e.g.,* White-Smith Music Publishing Co. v. Apollo Co., 209 U.S. 1, 19 (1908) (Holmes, J., concurring). *Cf.* Deep South Packing Co. v. Lathram Corp., 406 U.S. 518, 530-31 (1972) (patent accorded limited monopoly).

69. *Sony,* 104 S. Ct. at 784.

70.   In determining whether the use made of a work in any particular case is a fair use the factors to be considered shall include (1) the purpose and character of the use, including whether such use is of a commercial nature or is for nonprofit educational purposes; (2) the nature of the copyrighted work; (3) the amount and substantiality of the portion used in relation to the copyrighted work as a whole; and (4) the effect of the use upon the potential market for or value of the copyrighted work.

17 U.S.C. § 107.

Unfortunately, the new Act does little to explain "the most troublesome [doctrine] in the whole law of copyright." Dellar v. Samuel Goldwyn, Inc., 104 F2d 661, 662 (2d Cir. 1939).

71. Several fair uses are listed by the Registrar of Copyrights in the House Report: (1) "quotations of excerpts in a review or criticism," (2) "quotations of short passages in a scholarly or technical work, for illustration or clarification," (3) "summary of an address or article, with brief quotations, in a news report," (4) incidental reproduction in a news broadcast "of a work located on the scene of an event being reported," (5) "reproduction by a library of a portion of a work to replace a damaged copy," (6) "reproduction by a teacher or student of a small part of a work to illustrate a lesson," or (7) "reproduction of a work in legislative or judicial proceedings or reports." H.R. REP No. 1476, 99th Cong. 2d Sess., at 65, *reprinted in* 1976 U.S. CODE CONG. & AD. NEWS at 5678-79.

72. *Id.* at 66, *reprinted in* 1976 U.S. CODE CONG. & AD. NEWS at 5680.

codification of the fair use doctrine.[73] In many respects, the *Sony* decision may be determinative in the application of copyright law to home satellite viewing. The issue in *Sony* was whether Sony's sale of home video tape recorders to the general public violated any of the rights conferred upon Universal City and Walt Disney Studios by the Copyright Act.[74]

The district court held that copying of programming broadcast free of charge over the public airwaves constituted a fair use.[75] The Ninth Circuit reversed, strictly construing the Copyright Act and holding that home video recording was an infringement.[76] The Supreme Court reversed the court of appeals in a 5-4 decision:

> One may search the Copyright Act in vain for any sign that the elected representatives of the millions of people who watch television every day have made it unlawful to copy a program for later viewing at home, or have enacted a flat prohibition against the sale of machines that make such copying possible.[77]

An analysis of the Court's reasoning regarding home video recorders as a fair use will aid in understanding the possible concerns arising over satellite dish interception of pay cable signals.

The *Sony* Court examined each of the "factors to be considered" in § 107. This examination allowed the Court "to apply an equitable rule of reason analysis to [the] particular claims of infringement." The factors to be considered are: the purpose and character of the use, the nature of the copyrighted work, the amount of the work used, and the potential market impact of the use.[78]

The *Sony* Court used the § 107 factors to determine whether the use damaged the copyright holder. The Court described this damages test as follows:

> A challenge to a noncommercial use of a copyrighted work requires proof either that the particular use is harmful, or that if it should become widespread, it would adversely affect the potential market for the copyrighted work. Actual present harm need not be shown; such a requirement would leave the copyright holder with no

---

73. Although *Sony* considered the performance right (notes 52-59 *supra*), "its importance is tied to the breadth to be given the fair use doctrine." Piscitelli, *supra* note 3, at 14.

74. *Sony*, 104 S. Ct. at 777.

75. Universal City Studios v. Sony Corp. of Am., 480 F. Supp. 429, 456 (C.D. Cal. 1979), *rev'd in part*, 659 F.2d 963 (9th Cir. 1981), *rev'd*, 104 S. Ct. 774 (1984).

76. *Id.* The Ninth Circuit stated that previous judicial interpretation of the fair use doctrine "created doctrinal confusion that raises the spectre of the evisceration of the traditional working of the copyright scheme." *Id. at 971.*

77. 104 S. Ct. at 796.

78. 17 U.S.C. § 107.

> defense against predictable damage. Nor is it necessary to
> show with certainty that future harm will result. What is
> necessary is a showing by a preponderance of the evi-
> dence that *some* meaningful likelihood of future harm
> exists.[79]

Universal City and Walt Disney Studios did not carry the burden of showing
a likelihood of future harm. If the same test were applied to a hypothetical
case involving the use of a home satellite dish to intercept pay television
signals, a finding of unfair use would likely result.

a. Purpose and Character of the Use

Section 107(1) requires that the purpose and character of the use, including whether such use is of a commercial nature or is for nonprofit educational purposes, be examined. A commercial or profit-making purpose is
presumptively unfair.[80] However, the *Sony* district court's findings established that time-shifting,[81] the dominant use of the recorder, was a noncommercial activity.[82] It can be inferred from the *Sony* court's reliance on the fact
of free broadcast that the use of a satellite dish to intercept donation or
advertiser supported programs would also constitute a noncommercial
activity.

Pay cable originators such as HBO, however, receive part or all of their
revenue from subscribers.[83] Thus, intercepting those signals could be considered a commercial use because it dilutes the market for the copyright
holder's work. Indeed, Professor Lawrence H. Tribe's analogy that "jewel
theft is not converted into a noncommercial veniality if stolen jewels are
simply worn rather than sold,"[84] seems more appropriately applied to intercepted satellite signals than to home video recordings.

b. The Nature of the Copyrighted Work

The Court next considered "the nature of the copyrighted work."[85] The
Court held that viewing a televised, copyrighted, audiovisual work which
one had been invited to see "entirely free of charge" could be a fair use even

---

79. 104 S. Ct. at 793 (emphasis in original).

80. The Court said that "if the Betamax were used to make copies for a commercial or
profit-making purpose, such use would presumptively be unfair." *Id.* at 792.

81. Timeshifting is where a program is recorded so the viewer can watch at a more appropriate
time. The Court cited "televised sports events, religious broadcasts, and educational programs
such as *Mister Rogers' Neighborhood*" as examples of programs authorizing time shifting. *Id.* at
791.

82. "The use, limited to home recording and playback of audiovisual material *broadcast free of
charge* to Betamax owners over public airwaves, is noncommercial and does not reduce the market
for plaintiff's works." 480 F. Supp. at 456 (emphasis added).

83. *See supra* notes 9-10 and accompanying text.

84. 104 S. Ct. at 793 n.33 (quoting testimony before the Subcommittee on Courts, Civil Liberties
and the Administration of Justice of the House Committee on the Judiciary, 97th Cong., 2d Sess.,
Pt. 2, 1250 (1982)).

85. 17 U.S.C. § 107(2).

when seen at a time other than the broadcast time.[86] Viewers are not invited to see subscriber supported television free of charge. It is therefore unlikely that the Court could find that the nature and purpose of a pay television signal could allow its interception to be a fair use.

c. The Amount of the Work Used

Section 107(3) of the 1976 Act requires a court to consider "the amount and substantiality of the portion used in relation to the copyrighted work as a whole."[87] The *Sony* Court held that "the fact that the entire work is reproduced...does not have the ordinary effect of militating against the finding of fair use."[88] Satellite dishes can be used to view entire works broadcast on pay television. Absent the particular facts of home video recording, § 107(3) may prevent this use of home satellite dishes from being a fair use.

d. Potential Market Impact

The statutory phrase, "the effect of the use upon the potential market for or value of the copyrighted work,"[89] illustrates a major difference between home video recording and the use of home satellite dishes. The district court in *Sony* found that the use of home video recorders could possibly enhance the market for the copyrighted work in question.[90] The Supreme Court in *Sony*, however, held only that home video recording has "no demonstrable effect upon the potential market for, or value of, the copyrighted work."[91]

The *Sony* Court further suggests that to the extent timeshifting "expands public access to freely broadcast television programs, it yields societal benefits."[92] The Court concedes that the public interest in making television broadcasting more available[93] is not unlimited, but concludes that there must be some likelihood of harm before the "timeshifting" function of home video recorders will constitute an unfair use.[94]

Although home satellite dishes certainly expand public access to freely broadcast television programs, they also facilitate interception of pay television signals. The effect of satellite transmission on advertiser supported programs is not clear,[95] but satellite dish use is having an adverse effect on

---

86. 104 S. Ct. at 792-93.
87. 17 U.S.C. § 107(3).
88. 104 S. Ct. at 792-93.
89. 17 U.S.C. § 107(4).
90. 480 F. Supp. at 467.
91. 104 S. Ct. at 793.
92. *Id.* at 795 (emphasis added). The district court had noted that increasing access to television programing "is consistent with the First Amendment policy of providing the fullest possible access to information through the public airwaves." 480 F. Supp. at 454 (*citing* Columbia Broadcasting System, Inc. v. Democratic Nat'l Comm., 412 U.S. 94, 102 (1973)).
93. *See* Community Television of Southern Cal. v. Gottfried, 103 S. Ct. 885, 891-92 (1983).
94. 104 S. Ct. at 796.
95. *See supra* note 13.

subscriber supported broadcasts.[96]

Zealous attempts have been made to protect subscription television markets. In one year, ON-TV, the largest subscriber television operator, sued 56 companies for selling decoders used to unscramble the signal sent over the cable.[97] The pay television market, along with the service, will suffer as home satellite dish use becomes more widespread In this context, it is likely that a court would conclude that home satellite dish use would have a significant adverse effect on the market for the work.

Each of the four factors that Congress suggested the courts consider in their analyses indicates that the use of a satellite dish is, at least partially, an unfair use. The *Sony* Court's emphasis on "freely broadcast" programming that the public is "invited to see entirely free of charge" serves to highlight the unfair use associated with the interception of pay television broadcasts.

C. Liability under Section 605 of the Communications Act and the Cable Communications Policy Act of 1984

Section 605 of the Communications Act prohibits interception and publication of radio signals by unauthorized parties.[98] The Supreme Court has interpreted § 605 to give the Federal Communication Commission (FCC) authority to also regulate television broadcasts.[99] [100] Like copyright law, §

---

96. *See* Taylor, *Crossing Swords with the "TV Pirates"*, US NEWS & WORLD REP., May 25, 1981, at 65.

97. *Id.*

98. Section 605 provides:

> . . . No person not being authorized by the sender shall intercept any radio communication and divulge or publish the existence, contents, substance, purport, effect, or meaning of such intercepted communication to any person. No person not being entitled thereto shall receive or assist in receiving any interstate or foreign communication by radio and use such communication (or any information therein contained) for his own benefit or for the benefit of another not entitled thereto. No person having received any intercepted radio communication or having become acquainted with the contents, substance, purport, effect, or meaning of such communication (or any part thereof) knowing that such communication was intercepted, shall divulge or publish the existence, contents, substance, purport, effect, or meaning of such communication (or any part thereof) or use such communication (or any information therein contained) for his own benefit or for the benefit of another not entitled thereto. This section shall not apply to the receiving, divulging, publishing, or utilizing the contents of any radio communication which is transmitted by any station for the use of the general public, which relates to ships in distress, or which is transmitted by an amateur radio station operator or by a citizens band radio operator.

47 U.S.C.§ 605 (1982).

99. Congress did not contemplate cable television and satellite communications in 1934 when the FCC was established, but the Supreme Court has found cable television within the purview of the FCC. *See* United States v. Southwestern Cable Co., 392 U.S. 157, 168 (1968). Congress intended the Federal Communication Commission to be the single government agency regulating electronic communication. *See id. See also* American Broadcasting Co. v. FCC, 191 F.2d 492 (D.C. Cir. 1951), where the court stated that the purpose of Congress in establishing the FCC was to have an agency with the expertise to cope with the everchanging problems of a booming industry.

605 does not apply to tranmissions intended for the general public.[101] Although pay television is available to the general public, it is intended to be received only by those who pay for it. The issue of whether pay television is "intended for use by the general public" has been recently litigated.

A majority of courts hold that pay television is not intended for use by the general public and is therefore protected by § 605.[102] *Chartwell communications Group v. Westbrook* considered the legality of decoders used to unscramble intercepted pay television signals.[103] The court held that § 605 prohibited interception of such transmissions.[104] The court noted that unless pay television companies receive payment for their services they cannot survive financially.[105]

Furthermore, in the Cable Communications Policy Act of 1984, Congress created penalties for viewing scrambled programming through the use of illegal decoders.[106] However, the Act does not generally prohibit the interception of non-scrambled cable systems for home viewing.[107] The Act seems to preclude any liability under section 605 for home satellite dish viewing of non-scrambled systems.[108] Although one satellite dish user proclaimed that a "[f]ree lunch is legal now,"[109] the effect of the Act is to encourage satellite dish broadcasters to scramble their signals. The ultimate effect of the Act may thus be to leave satellite dish owners in the dark.

Although the media touted the new law as having "dispelled the legal

---

Enforcement actions can originate with the FCC. Courts have also held that a private cause of action may be brought under the Communications Act. *See, e.g.,* Chartwell Communications Group v. Westbrook, 637 F.2d 459 (6th Cir. 1980); Home Box Office, Inc. v. Pay T.V. of Greater New York, 467 F. Supp. 525 (E.D.N.Y. 1979); KMLA Broadcasting Corp. v. Twentieth Century Cigarette Vendors Corp., 264 F. Supp. 35 (C.D. Cal. 1967).

Because satellite signals are the logical extension of cable programming there is no reason to believe that the Court will not extend the regulatory powers of the FCC to satellite dishes as well. *See infra* notes 135-50.

100. *See supra* note 98.

101. *Chartwell,* 637 F.2d at 465.

102. *See* Chartwell Communications v. Westbrook, 637 F.2d 459 (6th Cir. 1980); Home Box Office, Inc. v. Pay TV of Greater New York, 467 F. Supp. 525 (E.D.N.Y. 1979). *But see* Orth-O-Vision v. Home Box Office, 474 F. Supp. 672 (S.D.N.Y. 1979). The *Ortho-O-Vision* holding has been characterized by one commentator as "bizzare." Perle, *supra* note 3 at 335.

103. 637 F.2d 459, 460-61 (6th Cir. 1980).

104. *Id.* at 605.

105. *Id.* at 465.

106. Cable Communications Policy Act of 1984, Pub. L. No. 98-549, § 5, 98 STAT. 2779 (1984). Unfortunately, the new Act provides for enforcement only through private litigation with a maximum recovery of $1,000 for noncommercial use of Decoders. The legal costs of enforcing the Act would probably outweigh the recovery.

107. Cable Communications Policy Act of 1984, Pub. L. No. 98-549, § 5(b), 98 STAT. 2779 (1984).

108. If the intercepted signal is used "for private financial gain," the dish owner is subject to a jail sentence of up to six months and a fine of up to $50,000. Cable Communications Policy Act of 1984, Pub. L. No. 98-549, § 5(d)(2), 98 STAT. 2779 (1984).

109. New York Times, Nov. 12, 1984, at 21, col. 1.

miasma that has shrouded the big dish antennas,"[110] that conclusion may be premature. The Act does nothing to clarify possible copyright infringement occasioned by satellite dish use. Arguably the new Act indicates a congressional intent to allow interception of pay television signals by satellite dishes. However, the Act includes no express intent to impact copyright law. Furthermore, the Cable Communications Policy Act is largely penal, whereas the Copyright Act is primarily compensatory. Therefore, the new Act should be interpreted as supplemental to the Copyright Act. The issue of how the Copyright Act applies to satellite dish interception is thus unresolved by the Act of 1984.

D. Vicarious Liability of Satellite Dish Manufacturers

If the use of satellite dishes infringes a copyright, the theory of vicarious liability provides a possible remedy.[111] In *Kalem Co. v. Harper Brothers*,[112] the Supreme Court held that the producer of an unauthorized film version of *Ben Hur* was liable for the sale of the film to "jobbers" who arranged for its commercial exhibition. The Court reasoned that the only use that could be made of the film was an infringing use.[113] Therefore, it found the producer liable for contributory infringement of copyright.[114]

In *Sony*, the Court found that the Betamax has many uses.[115] Although the Court conceded that some of the uses are infringing, it found that the primary uses are not. For example, timeshifting was found not to be an infringing use.[116] Also, some television programs are uncopyrighted and others may be copied without objection, and thus are not infringing. Since "the range of [the Betamax's] potential use is much broader than the particular infringing use of the film *Ben Hur* involved in *Kalem*," the court held that the "novel theory" of vicarious liability was insufficiently supported.[117]

The *Sony* Court's discussion of vicarious liability is particularly applicable to home satellite dishes. Like the Betamax, satellite dishes have a broad range of uses. Many of those uses, including the reception of signals intended for public use, are noninfringing. Therefore, although the interception of pay television broadcasts may be an infringement, the noninfringing uses probably will preclude a successful vicarious liability suit against a satellite dish manufacturer.

---

110. *Id.*
111. The theory of vicarious liability is utilized in almost all areas of the law. *Sony*, 104 S. Ct. at 785. Contributory infringement of copyright is "merely a species of the broader problem of identifying the circumstances in which it is just to hold one individual accountable for the actions of another." *Id.* In *Sony*, Universal City and Walt Disney Studios sought to hold Sony Corporation vicariously liable for the alleged infringement occasioned by the Betamax video recorder.
112. 222 U.S. 55 (1911).
113. *Id.* at 62-63.
114. *Id.* at 63.
115. 104 S. Ct. at 786.
116. *Id.* at 796.
117. *Id.* at 786.

II. THE INADEQUACY OF EXISTING LAW REQUIRES A CHANGE

Satellite dish users now can intercept broadcast signals without the consent of or compensation to the copyright holder. This is not a fair use of pay cable programs, whose broadcasters have not consented to the viewing of the broadcast by the general public and who rely upon paying customers for their compensation.[118] The Copyright Act of 1976, however, requires a strained application to provide a remedy.[119] A vicarious liability action against the product manufacturer would probably be unsuccessful.[120] Therefore, even if the interception is a copyright infringement, enforcement against individual satellite dish users would be prohibitively difficult and expensive. For the same reason, § 605 of the Communications Act is an unsatisfactory way to halt interception of pay television signals.[121] The current market solution to the interception of pay television signals is a stopgap remedy.

A. The Market Solution

Cable system operators have long recognized the inadequacy of current copyright law. A common method of protection is to scramble the cable signal and lease a decoder to the subscriber.[122] HBO has spent millions of dollars on plans to encode and decode its transmissions.[123] Those desiring to intercept the pay cable signals have fought the industry's technology with technology of their own. The battle of electrical engineers has left the would-be viewer with an ample supply of nonleased decoders.[124] As the scramblers become more sophisticated the decoders will likely keep pace.

So far, the decoder cases have been litigated under § 605 of the Communications Act.[125] The Cable Commmunications Policy Act of 1984 provides a new basis for attacking unauthorized decoding of intercepted satellite signals.[126]

State theft of services laws may provide another means of preventing the interception of non-scrambled signals.[127] Perhaps enforcement through state and local channels will be more economical than sifting through the existing federal copyright and communications law.[128] However, reliance on a

---

118. *See supra* notes 68-97 and accompanying text.
119. *See supra* notes 29-67 and accompanying text.
120. *See supra* notes 111-115 and accompanying text.
121. *See supra* notes 98-123 and accompanying text.
122. S. Robb, COMMUNICATIONS COURSEBOOK 5-13 (1978).
123. *See Anti-Piracy Move: Scrambling HBO*, BROADCASTING, Feb. 22, 1982, at 58.
124. *See generally* Taylor *supra* note 96.
125. *See, e.g., Chartwell*, 637 F.2d 459 (6th Cir. 1980).
126. Piscitelli, *supra* note 3, at 25.
127. Note: *supra* note 122, at 97. However, the Cable Communications Policy Act of 1984 may prevent the application of state theft of services laws to satellite dish use.
128. *Id.*

market solution enforced by state common law is inconsistent with the
federal intent to preempt copyright and communications law.[129]

B. A Legislative Solution

The 1976 Act's application to home satellite dishes is currently unclear.
The need for legislation in this area will increase as the impact of satellite
dishes on the pay television industry becomes more pronounced. The impact
is exacerbated by more technologically advanced satellite dishes available at
a lower cost.[130] In light of the increasing social and economic importance of
satellite dishes, Congress should enact new legislation.[131]

One suggestion is that § 605 of the Communication Act be amended to

---

129. 17 U.S.C., § 301 states:
> (a) On and after January 1, 1978, all legal or equitable rights that are equivalent
> to any of the exclusive rights within the general scope of copyright as specified by
> section 106 in works of authorship that are fixed in a tangible medium of
> expression and come within the subject matter of copyright as specified by
> sections 102 and 103, whether created before or after that date and whether
> published or unpublished, are governed exclusively by this title. Thereafter, no
> person is entitled to any such right or equivalent right in any such work under the
> common law or statues of any State.
> (b) Nothing in this title annuls or limits any rights or remedies under the
> common law or statutes of any State with respect to—
> (1) subject matter that does not come within the subject matter of copyright as
> specified by sections 102 and 103, including works of authorship not fixed in any
> tangible medum of expression; or
> (2) any cause of action arising from undertakings commenced before January 1,
> 1978; or
> (3) activities violating legal or equitable rights that are not equivalent to any of
> the exclusive rights within the general scope of copyright as specified by section 106.

The legislative history indicates that in enacting the 1976 Act, Congress intended to substitute "a
single Federal system for the present anachronstic, uncertain, impractical, and highly complicated
dual [state and federal] system." H.R. REP. No. 1476, 94th Cong. 2d Sess., 129, *reprinted in* 1976
U.S. CODE CONG. & AD. NEWS 5659, 5745.

The Supreme Court has held that in the Communications Act of 1934, as amended, "Congress
'formulated a unified and comprehensive regulatory system for the [broadcasting] industry.' "
Southwestern Cable, 392 U.S. at 168 (*quoting* Federal Communications Commission v. Pottsville
Broadcasting Co., 309 U.S. 134, 137 (1940)).

130. Lower cost has made home satellite dishes more readily available. *In re* Regulation of
Domestic Receive-Only Satellite Earth Stations, 74 F.C.C.2d 205, 207 (1979).

131. A common ground in the majority and dissenting opinions in *Sony* was the need for a
legislative answer to questions raised by the new technology of home video records. Justice
Stevens, for the majority said:
> It may well be that Congress will take a fresh look at this new technology, just as
> it so often has examined other innovations in the past. But it is not our job to apply
> laws that have not yet been written.

Sony, 104 S. Ct. at 796. Similarly, in his dissent Justice Blackmun stated:
> I would hope that these questions ultimately will be considered seriously and in
> depth by the Congress and be resolved there, despite the fact that the Court's
> decision today provides little incentive for congressional action.

Id.

Like home video recorders, home satellite dishes need legislative guidance. *See* Note, *supra* note
16 at 98; *but see* Piscitelli, *supra* note 122, at 37.

explicitly cover the interception of pay television by satellite dishes.[132] A better basis for enforcement would be to enact a new section of the Copyright Act, analogous to § 111, providing compulsory license fees for home satellite dishes. A license fee on the satellite dish and its components can be imposed in several ways.

A one-time fee could be paid upon the purchase of the satellite dish equipment. To adequately compensate the copyright holder, that fee would need to be substantial.[133] This type of approach could allow copyright holders to receive royalties through the Copyright Royalty Tribunal, as with compulsory licensing fees under § 111.[134] The thrust of legislation, however, should be to compensate the subscription television system operator directly because he has already purchased or leased the copyright. Fees should be prorated based on a market share, and the program creator would benefit indirectly through a higher price on the sale of his work.

Another approach to a compulsory license amendment would be to establish an annual assessment on the home satellite dish owner. The FCC asserted authority to license and did require licensing of all satellite dishes in 1970.[135] Apparently, the FCC decided that the regulation was impractical because, in 1979, it adopted a "voluntary licensing system."[136] An annual licensing fee may create enforcement problems that could be avoided through the use of a one-time fee.

---

132. *See* Note, *supra* note 122, at 99. By this theory, "Congress should expressly disallow the use of earth stations, even by private parties," because the financial effect on pay television companies could be devastating. *Id.* A tourniquet will stop a nosebleed if applied properly. Likewise, amending § 605 to outlaw satellite dishes will prevent pay television signals from being intercepted but will strangle a budding industry at the same time.

More appropriate, perhaps, is the possibility of amending § 605 to include and provide a means of enforcement against pay signal interception. In effect, this would make § 605 a federal theft of services law. A problem associated with this approach is the technical difficulty of allowing home satellite dishes to intercept only a given broadcast range. Considering the decoder technology, this problem may be so difficult as to render the law useless. Another drawback to such legislation is the need for door-to-door enforcement.

133. Piscitelli, *supra* note 3, at 39. As the cost of satellite dishes drop, the compulsory fee should increase to compensate copyright owners for the increased reception. This would keep the overall cost of the dish relatively stable.

134. *See* 17 U.S.C § 111(d).

135. First Report and Order, 22 F.C.C.2d 86, 99 n. 10 (1970).

136. First Report and Order, 74 F.C.C. 2d 205 (1979). The FCC noted that home satellite dishes "do not transmit radio signals and therefore cannot cause interference to other users of the radio spectrum." *Id.* at 218. Although the FCC concluded that licensing of satellite dishes was not mandated by the Federal Communications Act, it asserted "that the power to regulate receive-only earth stations is ancillary to our other regulatory responsibilities . . . ." *Id.* at 217.

137. Jerome H. Remick & Co. v. American Auto. Accessories, 5 F.2d 411, 411 (6th Cir. 1925).

III. CONCLUSION

When a burgeoning industry such as home satellite dishes taps into the existing home entertainment market some growing pains must be anticipated. Home satellite dish users unfairly enjoy the work of program creators and pay-television broadcasters by viewing pay television signals without payment.

The existing laws do not adequately protect copyrights from satellite dish infringement. "While statutes should not be stretched to apply to new situations not fairly within their scope, they should not be so narrowly construed as to permit their evasion because of changing habits due to new inventions and discoveries."[137] The Copyright Act of 1976 cannot be stretched to sufficiently protect the copyrights of creators from the unfair use of satellite dishes.

It is well within the capabilities of the free market system and the legislative powers of Congress to adapt to satellite television technology. Article I, Sec. 8 of the Constitution provides that:

> The Congress shall have the Power...to Promote the Progress of Science and useful arts, by securing for limited times to Authors and Inventors the exclusive Right to their respective Writings and Discoveries.

Congress has exercised that power by enacting the existing Copyright Act. Congress now has the responsibility to amend the current law to keep pace with the technology of the home satellite dish.

DANIEL J. WILKERSON

APPENDIX III

COPYRIGHT WARNING NOTICES

A. Warning Notice Required at Employee-Operated Copy Center

NOTICE

WARNING CONCERNING COPYRIGHT RESTRICTIONS

Reprinted from: *FEDERAL REGISTER*, November 16, 1977

APPENDIX III: COPYRIGHT WARNING NOTICES

B.   Copyright Notice Required to be Placed on all
     Copies Made by a Library Copy Center

**NOTICE: THIS MATERIAL MAY BE PROTECTED
BY COPYRIGHT LAW (TITLE 17, *U.S. CODE*).**

APPENDIX III: COPYRIGHT WARNING NOTICES

C. Suggested Warning Notice to be Posted at Unsupervised Copy Centers

NOTICE: THE COPYRIGHT LAW OF THE UNITED STATES (TITLE 17, *U.S. CODE*) GOVERNS THE MAKING OF COPIES OF COPYRIGHTED MATERIALS. THE PERSON USING THIS EQUIPMENT IS LIABLE FOR ANY INFRINGEMENT.

APPENDIX III: COPYRIGHT WARNING NOTICES

D.   Warning Label For Microcomputer Centers

JCCC POLICY
ON SOFTWARE COPYING

**Proprietary software packages
are protected by copyright laws.
DO NOT COPY without authorization.
To do so will make YOU liable for damages.**

THINK BEFORE YOU COPY!

Adhesive label attached to microcomputers at Johnson County (Kansas) Community
College.

APPENDIX IV

EDUCATIONAL CONSULTANTS AVAILABLE TO REVIEW COPYRIGHT POLICIES

Ivan R. Bender, Attorney
854 W. Cornelia, #201
Chicago, Illinois 60657
  (312) 248-5069 or (312) 256-4730

Don Hess
Media Center and Legal Copyright Consultant
Granite School District
360 E. Penny Avenue (3545 So.)
Salt Lake City, Utah 84115
  (801) 268-8076

Jerome K. Miller
Copyright Information Service
P.O. Box 1460
Friday Harbor, Washington 98250
  (206) 378-5128

Esther R. Sinofsky
Consultant/Instructional Design Specialist
1029 S. Orlando Avenue
Los Angeles, California 90035
  (213) 653-8917

Charles Vlcek, Director
Instruction Media Center
Central Washington University
Ellensburg, Washington 98926
  (509) 963-1221 or (509) 925-5484

SELECTED BIBLIOGRAPHY OF COPYRIGHT ARTICLES

This selected bibliography lists recent (1981-1985) publications dealing with copyright issues. The item marked with an asterisk is reproduced in this book.

COPYRIGHT: GENERAL

Ainsley, Lucy, *Presentation Kit for Principals* including overhead transparency master, script, and policy. $3.00. Order from Lucy Ainsley, Director of Instructional Technology, Birmingham Public Schools, 1525 Covington, Birmingham, MI 48010, (313) 644-9300, 1984.

Becker, Gary H., *The New Copyright Law*. Videotape. Available by sending a blank one-hour 3/4" or 1/2" VHS videotape, and $5.00 for duplicating and shipping (check payable to Seminole County Schools) to Gary H. Becker, Director of Media Services, Seminole County Schools, 1211 Mellonville Ave., Sanford, Fl 32771.

Brooks, Daniel T., *Fair Use of Educational Software*. Videotape. AECT, 1983. $120 to members, $150 to non-members.

Cronkhite, Jeannine, and Dell, Gary, *The Copyright Game Resource Guide*, 1983. $5.00 cash, $5.75 check or purchase order. Gary H. Becker, 1770 Blackman Court, Longwood, Fl 32779.

"Imagine a World Without." Free. Training Media Distributors Association, 1258 N. Highland Ave., Suite 102, Los Angeles, CA 90038.

Johnson, Beda, *How to Acquire Legal Copies of Video Programs*, 1985. Video Resources Enterprise, P.O. Box 191218, San Diego, CA 92119. $10 plus $1.00 for shipping and handling.

Johnson, Donald F., *Copyright Handbook, 2nd Edition*, New York, NY: R.R. Bowker Company, 1982.

Miller, Jerome K., *U.S. Copyright Documents: An Annotated Collection for Use by Educators and Librarians*, Libraries Unlimited, 1981. Out of print.

Miller, Jerome K., *The Copyright Directory*, 1985. $18 to non-profit libraries; $23 to others.

Miller, Jerome K., *Official Fair-Use Guidelines: Complete Texts of Four Official Documents Arranged for Use by Educators*. $5.95.

> Order the last two items from Copyright Information Services, P.O. Box 1460, Friday Harbor, WA 98250. Add $1.50 shipping and handling **per order**. $5.00 billing charge on billed orders under $15.

Olson, Lowell, "White Lightning - The New Prohibition," *Wilson Library Bulletin*, January 1982.

"Publishers, Librarians Debate Impact of Copyright Law," *Education Daily*, August 27, 1982.

Richardson, Alan, and Schwartz, Thomas, "What Media Managers Should Know About Copyrights," *Educational and Industrial Television*, October, 1982.

Sinofsky, Esther R., "A Report From the AECT Copyright Task Force On Copyright Issues," *Tech Trends*, May-June, 1985.

Sinofsky, Esther R., "Copyright in a Nutshell," *Instructional Innovator*, January, 1984.

Zirkel, Perry A., and Ivan B. Gluckman, "Copyrights and the Classroom," *NASSP Bulletin*, November, 1983.

U.S. Copyright Office, *Circular R1: Copyright Basics*

U.S. Copyright Office, *Circular R2: Publications on Copyright*

U.S. Copyright Office, *Circular R2b: Bibliographies, Selected*

U.S. Copyright Office, *Circular 21: Reproduction of Copyrighted Works by Educators and Librarians*

U.S. Copyright Office, *Copyright Act of 1976*.

> The U.S. Copyright Office pamphlets are free from U.S. Copyright Office, Information and Publications Section LM-455, U.S. Copyright Office, Library of Congress, Washington, D.C. 20559.

COPYRIGHT: TELEVISION

AECT, "Controversy Over 'Home Use Only' Labeling Leads to Statement of Clarification," *Access*, January/February, 1984.

"Beware of Unfair Videotaping," *American School Board Journal*, November, 1982, pp. 14, 16-17.

Hasper, David, "Receive-Only Satellite Earth Stations and Piracy of the Airwaves," *Notre Dame Law*, October, 1982.

Miller, Jerome K., "Copyright Considerations in the Duplication, Performance, and Transmission of Television Programs in Educational Institutions," *School Library Media Quarterly*, Summer, 1982.

Miller, Jerome K., *Using Copyrighted Videocassettes in Classrooms, Libraries, and Training Centers*, 2nd ed., 1986, $17.50.

Miller, Jerome K., *The Video/Copyright Seminar*, 1986, cassettes and documents. $24.75.

> The last two items may be ordered from Copyright Information Services, P.O. Box 1460, Friday Harbor, WA 98250. Add $1.50 shipping and handling per order. A $5.00 billing charge is added to **billed** orders under $15.00.

Powell, Jon T., "Guidelines for Off-Air Taping of Copyrighted Works For Educational Use," *Media and Methods*, March, 1983.

Singer, Sydnee Robin, "Satellite/Dish Antenna Technology: A Copyright Owners Dilemma," *Indiana Law Journal*, Vol. 59:417, 1984.

Sinofsky, Esther R., "Just When You Thought It Was Safe," *Instructional Innovator*, October, 1983.

Sinofsky, Esther R., Off-Air Videotaping in Education: Copyright Issues, Decisions, Implications. R.R. Bowker Co., 1985.

Troost, William F., "When To Say NO To Off-Air Videotaping," *Instructional Innovator*, January, 1985.

* Wilkerson, Daniel J., "The Copyright Act of 1976 Served on a Satellite Dish," *Willamette Law Review*, Winter, 1985.

COPYRIGHT: COMPUTERS

Bell, Trudy, "Copying Computer Software for Educational Purposes: Is It Allowed?" *Personal Computing*, November, 1983.

Bell, Trudy, "Copying Computer Software: What Risk, What Penalties?" *Personal Computing*, May, 1983.

Ehlinger, Cliff, "Copying Disks: The Why Not," *The Clearing: Newsletter of the Iowa Instructional Software Clearinghouse*, Spring, 1985.

Finkel, Leroy, "When Is a Pirate a Thief? The Moment He Makes His First Illegal Copy," *Electronic Learning*, October, 1983.

Helm, Virginia, *Software Quality and Copyright: Issues in Computer Assisted Instruction*. Book: ($13.50 to members, $16 to non-members). Videotape: ($90 to members, $110 to non-members), AECT, 1984.

Hess, Don, "Micro Computer Ethics," *On-Line Newsletter*, March, 1985, Utah Consortium for Information Technology in Education, 250 East 500 South, Salt Lake City, Utah, 1985.

"ICCE Policy Statement on Network and Mulitple-Machine Software," Available free from ICCE, 1787 Agate St., Eugene, OR 97403.

Miller, Jerome K., "Copyrighted Protection for Bibliographics, Numeric, Factual, and Textual Databases," *Library Trends*, Fall, 1983.

Pearlman, Dara, "Copy-Protection Controversies," *Popular Computing*, October, 1983.

Talab, Rosemary, "Look Both Ways Before You Copy Software," *Tech Trends*, February-March, 1985.

ABOUT THE AUTHOR

Charles W. Vlcek attended public schools in Eau Claire, Wisconsin. He has bachelor and master degrees in Industrial Arts (The Stout Institute, University of Wisconsin-Stout) and a doctorate in Educational Media (Michigan State University). He has been a secondary teacher and media coordinator in the Milwaukee and Eau Claire, Wisconsin, public schools. He is presently Director, Instructional Media Center, and Professor of Instructional Media, Central Washington University (past fourteen years) where he previously served as Television Coordinator (eleven years). He has held consultantships in Singpore and Malaysia for media building design.

Dr. Vlcek has written extensively in the media field and has been active in the copyright discussions for the past twelve years. He has served as a copyright consultant and speaker extensively in the Pacific Northwest and nationally.

INDEX

CURRENT AND FORTHCOMING PUBLICATIONS
FROM COPYRIGHT INFORMATION SERVICES

The Official Fair-Use Guidelines: Complete Texts of Four Official Documents Arranged for use by Educators. 32 pages. Paper cover. $5.95 Discounts available on sales of two or more copies.

Includes three Congressional fair-use guidelines, plus computer software guidelines issued by an educational association.

C.W. Vlcek, *Copyright Policy Development: A Resource Book for Educators.* Hardbound. 166 pages. $17.95

Provides step-by-step instructions for developing college and school district copyright policies and copyright manuals. Includes texts of several outstanding copyright policies and manuals.

J.K. Miller, *The Copyright Directory, Vol. 1: General Information.* 104 pages. Paperbound. $23. $5 discount to nonprofit libraries.

S. Strauss, *Copyright: A Practical Guide to Microcomputer Licenses.* 1986. 35 pages. Paper cover. $13.95

An excellent source of information about software licenses. The sample agreements in the appendix are written in plain English.

J.K. Miller, *Video/Copyright Seminar, 1987.* Audio cassettes, plus documents. $24.89 Reissued annually in the spring.

Prepared for school and college administrators, librarians, teachers, and media specialists. Treats videotaping off the air and using prerecorded videocassettes in classrooms and libraries.

J.K. Miller, *Computer/Copyright Seminar, 1987.* Audio cassettes, plus documents. $24.89 Reissued annually in the spring.

Prepared for school and college administrators, teachers, librarians, and media specialists. Treats duplication of software, networks, multiple boot-ups, and other computer issues facing educators.

J.K. Miller, *Using Copyrighted Videocassettes in Classrooms, Libraries and Training Centers.* 2d ed., available in 1987. $17.95.

Describes the impact of recent court cases. Treats using prerecorded videocassettes in classrooms and libraries, the effect of "home use only" labels, and licenses to perform videocassettes in classrooms, libraries, and college lounges. A new chapter treats video performances in hospitals, churches, offices, and industrial training centers.

Add $1.50 per order for shipping and handling.